For The Duration...

Edited by Angela Fairbrace

First published in Great Britain in 2009 by:
Forward Press
Remus House
Coltsfoot Drive
Peterborough
PE2 9JX
Telephone: 01733 890099
Website: www.forwardpress.co.uk

All Rights Reserved
Book Design by Ali Smith
© Copyright Contributors 2009
SB ISBN 978-1-84418-496-5

Foreword

Although we are a nation of poets we are accused of not reading poetry, or buying poetry books. After many years of listening to the incessant gripes of poetry publishers, I can only assume that the books they publish, in general, are books that most people do not want to read.

Poetry should not be obscure, introverted, and as cryptic as a crossword puzzle: it is the poet's duty to reach out and embrace the world.

The world owes the poet nothing and we should not be expected to dig and delve into a rambling discourse searching for some inner meaning.

The reason we write poetry (and almost all of us do) is because we want to communicate: an ideal; an idea; or a specific feeling. Poetry is as essential in communication, as a letter; a radio; a telephone, and the main criterion for selecting the poems in this anthology is very simple: they communicate.

Foreword

Although we are a nation of poets we are accused of not reading poetry, or buying poetry books. After many years of listening to the incessant gripes of poetry publishers, I can only assume that the books they publish, in general, are books that most people do not want to read.

Poetry should not be obscure, introverted, and as cryptic as a crossword puzzle: it is the poet's duty to reach out and embrace the world.

The world owes the poet nothing and we should not be expected to dig and delve into a rambling discourse searching for some inner meaning.

The reason we write poetry (and almost all of us do) is because we want to communicate: an ideal; an idea; or a specific feeling. Poetry is as essential in communication, as a letter; a radio; a telephone, and the main criterion for selecting the poems in this anthology is very simple: they communicate.

Contents

Robert W Lockett 1	Mollie D Earl 34
Keith Tissington 1	David Lin 35
Jennie Hope-Kirk 2	Daniel Beale 36
Dorothy Fuller 3	Catriona 37
Gilly Jones 4	Janet Cavill 37
Tracey Farthing 4	Yeside Ogunkoya 38
Mary O'Dwyer 5	Linda Bevan 38
Susan Prior 5	Doreen Furmston 39
Andrea Gillian Trick 6	Theresa Ann Sanderson 39
Kathy Johnson 7	Jeff Dipple 40
Janis Pope 8	Charles Harvey 42
Cheryl Taylor 8	Helen Dalgleish 43
Yvonne Shelmerdine 9	B McGrath 44
V King 9	Jane Brooks 45
Juliet Evans 10	Beryl Andrews 46
Karen Openshaw 11	Alan Whitworth 47
Derek Anthony Andrews 12	Pamela McCormack 47
Della Perry 13	Celia Caroline Layton 48
Jennifer Andrews 14	Ivana Cullup 49
Brenda Hughes 14	Catherine Armstrong 50
Kalbir Chahal 15	Colin Hush 50
Sharon Warren 15	Rev Barrie Williams 51
Ian Forsdike 16	Joy Elaine Mendez 51
Alan Ernest 17	Enid Crowhurst 52
Eunice Ogunkoya 18	Simon Cook 52
Gordon Ewbank 18	James Hazell 53
Sarah Dolan 19	Judy McEwan 53
Christopher Leith 20	Anton Nicholas 54
Heidi Penhallurick 21	Denis Martindale 55
Joanna Wooller 22	Colette Breeze 56
Sandra Rogers 23	Albert Bennett 57
O James 24	Julie Haggis 57
Valma June Streatfield 25	Kim Gourlay Almey 58
Stella Bush-Payne 26	Victorine Lejeune-Stubbs 59
Ronald Hiscoke 27	Annabelle Tipper 60
Daphne Fryer 28	Simone Farrugia Meiszner 61
Graham Watkins 29	Barbara Tozer 62
Margaret Rowe 30	Frank Tonner 63
Brian Hurll 31	Gordon Andrews 63
Robert D Hayward 32	Paul Kelly 64
Daniel White 33	Alasdair Sclater 65

Name	Page
Edgar Wyatt Stephens	66
Joyce Hudspith	67
Sheelah Collier-Ringer	68
Heather Pickering	69
Joan Hosker	70
Ann Voaden	71
Rosie Hinwood	72
Laraine Smith	72
John Willmott	73
Susan Mullinger	73
Samantha Rose Whitworth	74
Debra Ayis	75
Melanie Ann Calvert	76
Donna Salisbury	77
Muhammad Khurram Salim	77
Sheila Bates	78
Leonard A G Butler	79
Agnes Hickling	80
Edna Sparkes	81
Richard Muirhead	81
Geoffrey Speechly	82
Lucy Williams	83
Francis Page	84
Lesley Glendinning	85
Arthur Pickles	85
Lisa Cresswell Wilkinson	86
Laura Maxwell	86
Shelley Farr	87
Margaret Thompson	88
Lynn Elizabeth Noone	89
Finnan Boyle	90
Stella Mortazavi	90
Rachel Cross	91
Suzanna Wilson	92
Barbara C Perkins	93
Michael Hartshorne	94
Barbara Lambie	95
Caroline Foster	95
Bav	96
Sandra Softley	96
Taariq Crossley	97
Lorraine Jones	97
Nettie Thomson	98
Jeff Mearns	98
Mandi Evans	99
Oliver Cox	99
Christine Flowers	100
Pauline Uprichard	101
Lorena Valerie Owens	102
Gillian Morgan	103
Robert King	104
Eric Gladwin	104
P Dixon	105
Florence Greener	105
Stanley Moore	106
Anne Brodie	107
Liz Davies	108
Margot Reich	108
Kate Lyons	109
Janice Bailey	109
James Baxter	110
Clive Cornwall	110
Tony Beeby	111
Chloe Catlin	111
David North	112
Simon Foderingham	113
Lionel Brown	114
Val Haslam	115
K Lake	116
Christine Jean Venour	117
J B Watkinson	118
Natalie Williams	118
Danielle Ward	119
Rich rich Bard	119
Jennifer Mobley	120
Lillian Derry	121
Jessie Shields	122
Annette Foreman	123
Edna Ratcliffe	124
Tracey Cornwell	125
L J Roche	126
Brian Wharmby	126
Gillian Fitzsimmons	127
Anne Green	127
Debra Valley	128
Ryszard Lipinski	129
William Birtwistle	130
Philip Tucker	131
Christine Vincent	132
Margaret Parnell	133

Gordon Forbes	134
Cecil Hickman	134
Stephen Shutak	135
Jonathan Potter	136
Kimberly Harries	136
Awadhut M Shiwankar	137
Keith Miller	137
Maureen Beaumont	138
Stacey Wreford (14)	138
Jean McGovern	139
R N Taber	140
Carol Ann Lewis	141
Lesley S Robinson	142
Margaret Swan	143
Terry J Powell	144
Barbara Blackston	145
Elva Knott	146
Lisa Jane Mills	147
Paul Thackeray	148
Pamela Matthews	149
Anjum Wasim Dar	150
Soumyen Maitra	151
Helen Vesey	152
Margaret Pedley	153
Mabel (Deb) Moore	154
Lee Connor	155
Trudie Sullivan	155
Rosaleen Clarke	156
Shamim Ruhi	157
Audrey Faulkner O'Connor	157
J R Parkinson	158
M G Sherlock	158
Ann Dempsey	159
Yvonne Stevens	159
R O'Shaughnessy	160
Tessa Paul	162
Louis Cecile	163
Sylvia Wynne	163
Cyril G Payne	164
Margaret Kent	164
Jade Deacon	165
Milly Holme	166
Edna Rudge	167
Janet Thomas	168
Margaret Martin	169
Isabel Taylor	169
Dorothy Ellen Connor	170
Sheila Richford	171
Mahadi Kyeyune	172
Melissa Brabanski	173
V Fitzpatrick	174
Rachel Ritchie	174
Rosie Hues	175
Christopher Highton	175
Farina May Jenkins	176
Sharon Reed	177
M W Grainger	178
Pamela Javes	178
David Ryan	179
Paul A Taylor	180
Layla Hendow	180
Imogene Lindo	181
Umer Sharif	181
Sara Jane Berry	182
Esther Hawkins	182
Christopher Thomas	183
Peter Steele	184
Theresa Hartley-Mace	185
Leigh Smart	186
Sophie Jayne Mathews	187
Abigail Randall	188
Denise Edmonds	189
Rob Barratt	190
Shirley Sewell	191
Anne Gray	192
Yazmin White	193
Stuart Pickup	193
Amanda Prince	194
Peter Asher	194
Clare Furey	195
Alice Collins	195
Poppy Gooday	196
Gordon Jackson	198
Brenda Maple	199
Norma Fraser Reid	200
Marie Haswell	201
C M Lewin	202
J E Gobbin	203
Ray Duncan	203
Raymond Thomas Edwards	204

Patricia Turpin	205
Steven Hunter	206
Paola Borella	207
Phyllis Everett	208
Michelle Barnes	209
Gillian Fisher	210
Anita Marlene Stridgen	210
Robert Bradley	211
Adam Imaan	212
Ade Horton	212
J M White	213
Mr G Watkins	214
June Holmes	215
Valerie Tedder	216
B J Shire	217
Roger Oldfield	218
Arthur S Waller	219
Erica Warburton	220
Patrick Joseph Ryan	220
Dorothy M Titley	221
Robert Shreeve	221
Robin R Robinson	222
Marje Dale	223
Shirley Brooks	224
Lucy Mary Dean	225
Barry Ryan	226
Jennifer Clare Kerr	227
Angy Lindsay	227

The Poems

I Have Loved You My Love

I have loved you my love,
With a love that dies not in time,
Or with the heart's capriciousness,
But in my soul precious to myself
There have I loved you.
And in this love no falsehood ever rises,
But growing fonder by the years
Excludes the boldest fears.
For you who sealed the ducts
And made my eyes to glisten
Like the dew upon the webs
That is seen by early rising
Are my love's far flung horizon
Ever seen and ever compassed in my soul.

Robert W Lockett

Anniversary

The world turned and the year passed
And our hearts, they remained steadfast.

Like a fossil remains forever
Preserved in rock for all to see.
You and I remain together
Me preserved in you,
And you in me.

The flame lit by our heart's desire
Still burns strong and ever higher.

The light it gives still shows the way
Down devotion's ever winding road.
To this, another anniversary day,
The remembered ember,
Of when our love first glowed.

Keith Tissington

Nothing But The Truth

I've been twisting in madness, hoping to find
Reasons for this, silence of mind
Grasping at notions: slipping away
Silently pleading for love to stay,
Cradling anger, here in the hands
That polish the anger: part of the plan
I'm reaping the timing, sewing it shut
You've always known that it isn't enough.
Falsify reasons, to push me away
So you don't have to want me to stay
Catch me: I'm falling, harder than stone
Do not wish for better, or pull me undone.
You know I love you, acknowledged too well
The very reason, we won't ask for help.
I'll leave you tomorrow, as bitterness bites
Down on the anguish that forced me to fight.
In separate darkness, our hearts make plans
To synchronise actions we don't understand
Call me in the morning so I hear you say
I miss you, darling, tomorrow, today.
Thrive on the teardrops staining our feet
To make me feel I have to compete
Your eyes are glazed in all I don't know
Just where was it that you lost your way home?
Reach for my hand and I'll teach you to fight,
Each of the demons that prowl in the night
Retrace the feelings, yes: it will hurt
But please take this chance, we'll reap in its worth.
Move on from the pain, of who did you wrong
If you're ever to see that, yes, we do belong.

Jennie Hope-Kirk

For The Duration . . .

My Man

I first met my man when I was fifteen
He'd lovely red hair, face shaven clean
Although a builder who worked in the dirt
He always dressed smart, suit, tie and shirt.
We've been together for fifty odd years
We've had wonderful times, much laughter and tears
He still touches my bum each time he passes
The thought of sex still steams up his glasses.
Not much red hair now, nearly all white
But I still think he's a bit of all right
He still makes me smile when he appears
Can make me laugh or move me to tears.
We laugh together when recalling the past
I don't know how much longer we will last
But it's been a truly remarkable life
I'm still so proud that I'm his wife.
I love every bit of him from his funny shaped toes
All the way up to the bumps on his nose
He can't walk very fast now, he's much slower
And his middle-aged spread is sinking lower.
His eyes still blue, just a little bit dimmer
Both of us could be a little bit slimmer
But we fit together like bread and cheese
And we both have the same arthritic knees.
I loved him then and I love him still
Whilst we are together I always will
He comforts me like a very warm glove
After all these years we are still in love.

Dorothy Fuller

The Gift Of Love

A face peered out of a blanket of wool,
Eyes wide open, such a face you did pull,
Suddenly you started to wail and to cry,
A sound that stopped as I held you close by.

My tiny baby, you were a delight,
When I held you everything seemed just right.
But before long a toddler you'd become,
I'd hear your little voice calling me, 'Mum.'

I give you all my love, my darling one,
The days of childhood are so quickly gone,
Time has raced by, and although you have grown,
You're still the best child that I've ever known.

Now you are older and know your own mind,
Sometimes you bring me flowers which is kind,
But when, 'I love you,' are words that you say,
It's the best gift of all that comes my way.

Gilly Jones

Love Unexpected

Love unexpected, love always mine,
Love to share with thee divine.
Love conquers all through battles hard,
Where times are troubled and often marred.
Love seeks answers that come and go,
Love's all around and people know.
The happiness that love brings to us,
And where comfort is needed, love makes a fuss.
Love so pure, and love divine,
Love conquers all, love entwined.

Tracey Farthing

To Someone Special

Try not to grieve, now that I have gone.
Gaze at the stars, the moon, the flowers;
I'm all around you, protecting you like the sun.
Try not to count the seconds, the minutes, the hours.
I am not perfect, don't think of me like this.
I am a mere mortal passing through your life.
All my kind words and deeds won't go amiss.
Keep yourself together, keep yourself safe.
Remember, I love you too, the whole heart of you.
We had something very special together.
I just want to let you know that I miss you too.
I'll be watching over you whatever the weather.
I am your guardian angel, sent from above.
I blow you soft kisses, so deep is my love.

Mary O'Dwyer

Children

With three I'm blessed, and each so fair
And all my love is there to share
Each one so different, each one so rare.

My Sarah first with looks so stunning
With talent and love that's overflowing
From childhood Dance with medals glowing
To travelling the skies, her dreams still growing

My Chris with his kindness and laid back air
His nature so sweet and his love always there
His aims are much lower but failures are rare
Dear Chris you're a winner, without a care.

Then there's the younger so big and so tall
Sport is his love and he'll hit any ball
He's funny and clever, he's certainly no fool
Dear Simon our baby who goes for it all.

Susan Prior

Motherhood

The role of motherhood
Is a daunting task
They take you for granted
And don't always ask!
You bring them home for the very first time
Don't speak too loud, you learn to mime.

The first time they cry
You jump to your feet
Warm up their bottle
And check on the teat.

Feeding and changing is all you do
What's this in their nappy?
This green and black glue!
The first time you bathe them
They're as slippery as soap
Oh where is that midwife
I really can't cope!

To change their clothes is a task on its own
What's wrong with these armholes
Have they been sewn!

At last you get them off to sleep
But every ten minutes you have a peep.
Checking that they're safe and sound
That little creation all snugly bound.

Andrea Gillian Trick

For The Duration . . .

My Grandson Lewis

A very hot summer's day was nearly ended,
When you were born, I attended.
I cut the cord that had nourished you,
A difficult birth, you were just a little bit blue,
Mummy was exhausted, Daddy as well,
I held you and came under your spell.

You looked at me with such a knowing look,
Grandad, some lovely pictures he took.
A bond had been forged between us so strong,
You know what is right and dislike any wrong.
Lewis always senses when I am unwell,
Feeling tired and aching, Lewis can tell.

You quickly grew almost every day,
Soon it was time for your first birthday.
I baked a cake in the shape of Winnie the Pooh,
Your little friends came to share it with you.
The years passed quickly, you are almost eleven,
And Curtis, your brother, has just turned seven.

Moments with my grandson are ones to treasure.
Time in his company is a lasting pleasure.
I hope to see him when he is grown,
Maybe he will have a family of his own.
Lewis, we are proud of you, we love you dearly,
Your eyes show love, reflected so clearly.

Kathy Johnson

Memories

It's been twelve long months today
Since the angels came and took you away.
No words could ever really explain
Our innermost feelings of loss and pain.

You filled our hearts and dwelling place
Now there is only an empty space.
A loving smile, a gentle touch
We all miss you and love you so much.

You promised you would be with us forever
And we won't forget my love, not ever.
A perfect Dad, a loving partner
For us there will never be another.

We will carry you forever in our heart
And when our time comes to depart.
You will rise once more to quell our pain
Because in Heaven on Earth, we will meet again.

Janis Pope

The Fox And The Rabbit

Emily Eccles was all of a dither
For Sir Henry Devour had asked her for dinner
Should she wear blue with a white lace trim
Or her Sunday best smock, matching hat with wide brim?
But alas poor Emily was entering a trap
As the grand Sir Henry was far from that
Overwhelmed by his looks, cunning charm and appeal
It soon became apparent poor Emily was the meal
So don't be fooled by grand titles and dress
For it's what lies within that should really impress.

Cheryl Taylor

For My Remarkable Children

When you feel lost in a crowd
I will carry you on my shoulders
And whisper words of encouragement
If you are losing heart.

When you are tired
Lay down - I will stroke you,
And if you are lonely
I will keep you company.

Always know this:
When you need me - I am there -
At your achievements
My heart will burst with pride;
I will dance at your wedding,
And when your children are born
My tears of joy will fall on their faces.

Keep my soul in your heart;
This is my gift.
Let it shine
And you will never be alone.

Yvonne Shelmerdine

My Grandaughter

The life I have lived has made me happy,
Made things all worthwhile to see the little smiling face
Of my darling grandchild,
Pray God give her the happiness
And the love that brought her here,
To live her life with someone
Who will forever hold her near.

V King

The Post Office

The village post office is never still
It stands at the bottom of a very steep hill
It is owned by old Mr Fry
A very prim man, but extremely shy,
Completely different from his wife
Who's never blushed in all her life
As different as chalk and cheese, they are
But very nice to know, by far.

Although she gossips much too much
If someone comes in they'll miss their lunch
If only to hear of the cats next door
That made their nest in a hole in the floor
Mrs Fry knows everybody
The prim, the proper and very shoddy
Mrs Fry knows everything
All the gossip she will bring.

The letters she sorts take all day
Every morning there's a delay
Because she reads all the addresses
What's in the letters, she often guesses
Her glasses propped upon her nose
Counting stamps as she goes
The beans fall off, the tins fall over
The cabbages in boxes, sent from Dover.

Tins of fruit and tins of meat
All the shelves kept tidy and neat
Boxes of paper and boxes of soap
Stationery and string and rope
Bottles of Coke and bottles of wine
Powder and polish to make the place shine
The counter where you bring your letter
And buy a stamp to make it better.

When the last person of the day
Has bought her food and gone away
When all the letters have been collected
And payments made have been corrected
The sign on the door is put to 'closed'

And Fry and Mrs have had a nose
To check the shop and turn off the light
Then they're ready to go home for the night
Rested for the next day when all is new
To do the work they always do
To sell and profit to the good
That village post office, like it should.

Juliet Evans

Being Apart

We've been apart now for most of my life,
You couldn't be there to see me as a wife.
I needed you most at the birth of my girls
They're beautiful Mum - though neither have curls!

You left me protected; in love's tender care
Johnny and Anne have always been there.
We've all done OK, my brothers and me,
The pain in their eyes not many would see

They say time's a healer and this may be true
But time couldn't replace a mother like you
There are tears in my eyes as I write down this verse.
Being apart - it's been my life's curse.

But I feel you watch over when we're all having fun;
Bathe in your love in the warm, summer sun.
You're there when I'm sad - you're there when I smile,
Thoughts of your presence help with life's trials.

Mum, even though death has ripped us apart;
You'll live on forever - right here - in my heart.

Karen Openshaw

Heartbeat

You are my heartbeat
Stronger than what I eat
Better than sugar beet
Healthier than wheat
My love for you is extremely sweet
From the first day we meet

Honey, loving you is better than money
Sweeter than honey
Together you and I are full of laughter so funny

Our journey is unending
And forever resounding
Always maturing in knowing
And growing

You are my heartbeat
Loving you is my meet

I am satisfied and full
From the treasures of my heart to you
Every day, every year spent with you is anew

A wife so fair and a mother who is always there
Whom I love with every care and is dear
I appreciate you more than you know so let's take things slow,
That we may continue to grow.

Derek Anthony Andrews

Shells

Stepping along the golden sand
Stooping to collect pink and beige shells
Took me straight back to my youth
When we did this together
It always seemed sunny when we were on holidays
It was always a joyous time
Mostly because you were there too
What changed? We grew to be adults
With families of our own and jobs
No time for each other anymore
Not because we don't want to, because of time
The sun doesn't shine so often now
We are preoccupied with surviving.
The sand smells putrid nearer the sea
But it feels like coming home
It is familiar to me
I miss hearing our laughter running through the froth,
Young and carefree.
I pick up the shells, run them through my fingers
Place them in a tiny bag
I watch my own boys playing, laughing
Carefree, young and I am jealous of them
I wish we didn't have to grow up
But we do, time rolls in like the ocean's tide
Pulling us along with it
Now it is their time
Ours is but memories.

Della Perry

Baby Love

I felt an instant mother's love
For the one sent from above
A token of joy and liberty
The one who was born to me

The moment she was placed in my arms
I was immediately struck by her charms
Her rosy cheeks, the twinkle in her eyes
All spoke to me of a beautiful sunrise

I look around, how can it be?
Time has gone by all too fleetingly
First smile, first word, first step all passed
How I wish it could have last

Once bright smiles and laughter, *hee hee hee*
From one so young, innocent and free
But no longer dependant, now fully grown
My baby love now has her own.

Jennifer Andrews

Julia

J esus uses love in all
U sing simple people
L iving ordinary lives
I nspiring by example
A ll-embracing love

M assaging and touch skills
O ffering consolation
R eassuring words and hugs
R eady wit and humour
O ur beautiful friend
W e cherish your memory.

Brenda Hughes

Wishing Of Childhood

Wouldn't it be great if life was always fun
Running around playing in the sun
Splashing in puddles with wellies in the rain
No worries or cares in the world, wouldn't it be great!

Living in a world where magic exists
I can be a fairy or dragon, anything I wish!
In my own little world I can go anywhere I want to be
From high in the sky to deep in the sea.

There's always laughter and cheer where I go
Life is so great only I know,
Isn't it a pity as adults we can't have the same fun
Wouldn't it be great to be a child again!

Kalbir Chahal

Why?

Death eventually happens to us all,
But when it's someone close, who gets the call,
The fear, the hate, your hurting inside,
A thousand things run through your mind.

Why us? Why now? How can this be?
The illness is over, but you can't see,
Why it has happened to one of your own,
You run and hide, and want to be alone.

You try and find someone to blame,
But you know things will never be the same,
They say time heals and the pain goes away,
But you remember them each and every day.

You reminisce about the good and the bad,
But although sad, you feel very glad,
That the person who used to hold your hand,
Has moved onto a better land.

Sharon Warren

Celestial Concert

Ejected from the Sun, charged particles race,
Coming at us, unstoppable, across darkest space.
Where, channelled to the Poles by Earth's magnetic field;
They glow high in our protective air shield.

Aurora Borealis, the Northern Lights,
Are majestic performances played through the night.
The heavenly arena, set way above our heads,
Is lit by sheets of vaporous greens and reds.

The ghostly ensemble works the stage on high,
Throwing curtains of light across the sky;
But few see the show, the acts are too fleet,
Gazes are downward, fixed firmly at their feet.

Back and forth the spectral lights play,
Never to be seen by the light of day.
Night's phantom radiance, the astral dance,
Is a random stellar presence, formed by chance.

But, too soon, the concert fades from our eyes,
Guttering and shimmering it fails, then dies.
The silent beauty takes its bow at height;
Encore the celestial player of the night!

Ian Forsdike

A Friendly Invitation To A Scientific Basis For Creation

Sometimes my pursuit of all aspects of the uncanny takes me abroad - such an occasion has now arisen: The spectre of a large black cat, prowling the outskirts of a small town in Holland has given the Dutch tabloids a field day - knowing of my special interest in such spectres my specialist friend invites me to stay and investigate the phenomenon.

As I step down from Euro-train he greets me with a cheery smile. The moustache is a little greyer since last we met, but otherwise there is little difference - the weight perhaps - has decreased over the intervening year, which, if anything, now seems more natural. Drawing near he shakes my hand; leads me towards his parked car, hoping I may feel a good deal heartier once I partake of refreshments in his humble apartment home.

Depositing a CD in the TV he exhorts, 'This - will explain everything - note the dates - the times, . . . Look hard . . . ! Then look hard again! - Take a good look at what you see.'

Now it became all too obvious: despite being recorded miles apart - in two scenes the dates and times were identical: How could a metaphysical animal propel itself with sufficient high velocity across such a wide expanse - without first dematerialising then materialising and sinking under the weight of its own projected mass . . . !!

I made my way hurriedly homeward towards the one opportunity he so avidly sought - the chance to see if his concepts were correct - that this beast could be generated to telepathically cross-oceans; bonding with the mind - His mind; - The brainchild of its creation.

Alan Ernest

Creativity

Creativity is designing
Shapes and colours to create forms,
Materials and technology for texture.
Enhance with function for different styles!

Creativity is composing
Notes and beats to create music,
Words and language for creative writing.
Evoke emotion with various genres!

Creativity is evolving
Scents and perfumes to create moods,
Ingredients and methods for recipes.
Spice up with fashion for different trends!

Eunice Ogunkoya

Untitled

Singing
Not dancing,
Not calling out a name.
A cause,
A cancer of remembering and shame.
Shame of promises kept or lost,
Shame of forgetting.
Maze of feeling,
Sun blind behind the haze of days
And nights
When you and I are close, yet
Not dancing.

Gordon Ewbank

Of Maps And Men . . .

Back then I was a worrier
I never liked to roam
I didn't like the travelling
But preferred to stay at home

I couldn't read directions
I was useless with a map
I couldn't tell my left from right
Which got me in a flap

But now my life is different
In fact, I've seen the light
Although he's only small and black
To me he's 'Mr Right'

He doesn't give me aggro
He just tells me where to go
He never ever scolds me
Or says I drive too slow

He never tries to leave me
And doesn't stay out late
And when I've had enough of him
I can change his name to 'Kate'

He looks good on my dashboard
I like to turn him on
I slip us into first gear
And *whoosh* you find me gone

So ladies don't be fretful
Don't lock yourselves away
Go out and buy a sat nav
And burn your maps today!

Sarah Dolan

Mara

Mara is one of my workmates
He's the best around this place
And whenever you happen to see him
He's got a smile across his face

He's a big 'hairy arsed' man's man
And he does some 'real man's' stuff
He has played football for Scotland
Where he proved he is good enough

When his dear Dad was sadly taken
The grief almost put him off the rails
But with his mum's love and understanding
Managed to get his boat 're-sailed'

He was accepted into Aberdeen Uni
Stuck in but still got into all the pranks
Then he got a scholarship in America
To teach football to the Yanks

He started here two years ago
And always has stood out
Working away quietly and steadily
With no need to scream or shout

He has a need to keep on learning
And always says, 'How can this be?'
And with his continual thirst for knowledge
He's destined to 'top the company tree'

If anyone happens to be struggling
And are obviously needing a hand
Because he is so knowledgeable
They know that 'Mara is their man'

His bachelor days are nearly over
He's about to give up his single life
As the very lucky Jenny
Is about to be his lovely wife

So of all my working colleagues
Mara is by far the best
His knowledge, smiles and frendliness
Puts him miles above the rest.

Christopher Leith

Wind Blows The Chimes
(In loving memory of Conner Penhallurick born and died on 6th July 2003)

When I feel the wind blow in my hair
And the thousand wind chimes dancing there
That's when I feel my son is there

Blow the wind chimes softly
With the music you make
We will see all our children dancing there
That's a vision we must take

I hold my hand out to you
Please do not take
Your job is to blow the chimes
For the music you must make.

Heidi Penhallurick

70th Birthday Mum!

70th birthday Mum!
It doesn't seem quite true.
We only have to take a walk
And can't keep up with you!

You never sit quite still for long,
Always 'on the go'
WI, yoga, walking
Dashing to and fro.

We all can be heard saying,
Where have those years all gone?
But we have memories to treasure
Some good, some sad, some fun.

We don't forget our 'loved ones'
Who sadly can't be here
But we know they watch us daily
We remember them so dear.

With your family all around you
We hope we've made you proud.
We have enjoyed the weekend,
Last night though . . . Far too loud!

So with a Super-Dooper 'Bruising Nudge'
We send our love to you -
Hoping you have had a 'real fab time'
Let's sit back and down a few.

Joanna Wooller

For The Duration . . .

The Sunshine Flower

The sunshine flower shines from her pretty painted pot
From behind the greenhouse window she watches stifled and hot.
She is golden and she is yellow for she is watered and she is fed
She watches the sun set behind the garden shed
Golden and red

Oh sunshine flower smile for me
Behind your glass for only one to see.
She sits, she waits, she smiles, she lingers
On the one who tends with the caring green fingers.
One to one and then he's gone.

The sunshine flower is radiant and bright
She takes from her roots, the air and the light.
But what of the love tendered gentle and kind?
And what of her smile, maybe something behind?

Behind her smile however alas,
There are thoughts of wild fields and luscious green grass
She longs to dance in the breeze where the gypsy grass grows,
Free spreading seeds with the larks and the crows.
Longing to feel the wind and the rain
She bows her head and feels her pain.

Oh sunshine flower smile for me,
Behind your glass for only one to see.
She sits and she waits and she smiles and she lingers,
On the one who tends with the caring green fingers.

Sandra Rogers

The Snow At Last

The day before
So cold, so windy
The wind was blowing
So strong and icy
It turned our brollies inside out.

The tears ran down
As I squint and shout
'Hold on tight
Or you just might
Lose everything
In the flash of a light.'

That night no rain
But extra cold
Who knows what the morning
Will behold.

As we awake
It seems so bright
Guess what's happened
During the night?
The snow is finally
On the ground
So crisp and fresh
And glistening all around.

O James

The Lone Star
(Written for my teenage Granddaughter, Melissa)

Pretty and talented,
A joy to behold -
Singing and dancing
With steps - oh so bold,
Always the mimic
In accents so clear,
Helping the migrants
To speak and to hear.
A darling with babies
Of whom there are seven
Meeting her cousins -
A stairway to Heaven.
Wonderful actress -
A star to the core,
Especially with Shakespeare,
The stories of yore.
Lady MacBeth was the part she last played,
Fully professional,
Not a slip had she made,
Just like the original.
She's right at the top -
At least in my own eyes
Now *where* will she stop?

Valma June Streatfield

Childhood Memories

From a young farming family of five,
I was the first born girl to arrive,
On a Sunday lunchtime, 12th October,
To Weeford Road Farm, the midwife pedalled over.

With cows and horses, chickens too,
My parents were kept busy, now with me, it's true,
Milk to deliver to customers everywhere each day,
Horse and float with a milk churn - Dad filled jugs that way!

Then one summer's day First Prize I won
At a Baby's Competition, entered in fun.
Soon twin sisters were now on the way,
So to London, Gran took me back with her to stay.

When walking in London Big Ben looked so tall,
But then of course I was still quite small,
A big bustling city, beautiful parks so green,
River Thames, Tower Bridge, Royal Processions seen.

Gran sometimes took me to the seaside at Southend,
To meet my Godmother and her friend.
We saw fish just caught, fresh from the sea,
Crabs, cockles and mussels, and pink rock, was for me!

At five years to a local school went I
Where nursery children on little beds did lie.
To receive piano lessons from a lady Gran knew,
We walked past a newspaper printers, very noisy too!

For my little hands to stretch an octave was a real test,
Gran made me persevere, I did my very best,
When Grandad retired as a chef we moved from the flat,
Now seven years old said a goodbye to London
Joining family on another farm -
Another life - another story -
And that's that!

Stella Bush-Payne

Baby It's You

It was so difficult to bring you into this world
All the pain and suffering was worth it, my joy all seems absurd
You have brought such happiness as we are now so close
That dearest darling baby boy, it's no wonder that I boast
Concerned were the medical staff as you prematurely arrived
Immediately placed in an incubator where you thrived
I visited you daily as your progress was maintained
I held my little baby, to me it was very strange.

Responsive and alert you whimpered, I knew our bond had formed
So tiny and so precious, your little limbs had formed
Soon you gathered strength and no longer required intensive care
I was allowed to care for you with tenderness I prepared
We bought you home all marvelled, I supervised your show
Respecting the hospital's instructions you then steadily did grow
Upon those many health checks all are amazed you so wondrously well.
Thank God you are responding, I love you, none can tell

Your brothers and sisters gaze at you, they are warned,
'Do not touch'
Like a little pixie you lay in your cot, admired so much
Caring for you continually you respond when we recite your name
Dreaming in those baby dreams as you thrive and gain
So many good wishes which are prized as you open your baby-blue eyes
A little whimper and the signs of a tear and I prepare you loving care
So cherished and loved a gift so wondrously conceived
It was worth all that anxiety, we the parents are so proud indeed.

Ronald Hiscoke

For Mollie

What a perfect little baby
A joy for all to see
Bringing with you happiness
Especially for me
You were the best one
That came into my life
After Grandad died
Giving me a lot of strength
With which my tears to hide
There will be other babies
Maybe quite a lot
But you my darling Mollie
Will hold a special spot
Your bright blue eyes light up
When perchance we meet
With arms thrown open wide
And a huge great hug to greet
So my hopes and dreams for you
Are that life gives you the best
Of everything you ever want
Because to me my darling Mollie
You are the best.

Daphne Fryer

For The Duration . . .

Baby It's You

Life assumed a glorious hue,
Gazing upon a bonny wee bundle
One to cuddle and fondle
God's blessing on man and wife,
Pure pink evidence of new life
Together they said, it's all due to
Baby it's you.
You are a gorgeous sensation
Truly a heavenly creation, to cherish
By a deliriously happy dad and mum.
Peering into its cradle, saw
An armful of future,
A child to love unto kingdom come.
Destined this world to renew,
Of course, baby it's you.
A symbol bright as fine weather,
In your parents' cap a striking feather.
Seeing you sound asleep is
A memory forever to keep,
Even if struck blind, it would be
Easy to picture you in the mind.
Yes, baby it's you who'd
Command our third eye view.

Graham Watkins

First Grandchild

I'm going to be a granny!
That's music to my ears.
Holding a grandchild in my arms,
The thought brings me to tears.

Will it be a boy or girl?
I really do not care.
With a history of twins
Perhaps they'll have a pair!

I'm getting all excited
Thinking of what we'll do.
Reading a bedtime story,
Maybe a trip to the zoo.

Building sandcastles on the beach
And paddling in the sea.
Catching little baby crabs
And then back home for tea.

Kicking a ball about the park
And sitting on a swing.
Being cosy in a chair
With nursery rhymes to sing.

Hearing the name of Granny
From a little smiling face.
Seeing you at school one day
And tying your first shoelace.

I have a few months left yet
For the dream to linger on,
And waiting for the phone call
From a proud and happy son.

Margaret Rowe

Baby It's You

Our family is having more happy times,
Mutual love is in the air.
Our forty-year-old got married,
And is in love, without a care.
We had a lovely wedding
Near a forest leafy glade
Lots of glorious smiles
At this function were displayed.
Then in toddled Olivia,
She's our granddaughter you know.
Thirty inches of beautiful child,
And a smile, enough to make you glow.
She is our little angel eyes.
Her sparkle is wonderful to see
When we see these two together
We know what their future will be.
Auntie and niece, all love and peace,
They have a lovely bond,
Dawn is dark and beautiful, too
Ollie is two, and a curly blond.
We are so proud of my family,
United we stand, for all time.
Our son sits in total amazement,
Knowing this family love is sublime,
Ollie has triggered the future,
Dawn has found a little, new friend
Even if I meet my maker,
I know that this love will not end.

A happy grandad
Brian.

Brian Hurll

A Special Friend

I have a special Friend
Who lives forever;
He is not light or fickle
Like human beings,
But lives in blinding light
In highest Heaven.

And yet this special Friend
Dwells in my heart
Through His Holy Spirit
Poured into my soul;
And I know He will never
Leave or forsake me.

This Friend came to Earth,
Born in a feeding trough
Amongst farm animals,
Because there was no room
For Him in the inn.
He was the Christ Child

Born to be the Saviour
Of the world; and yet
He was Himself God -
God as a human being.
He gave sight to the blind,
Cured all diseases

And healed the sick,
Making the deaf hear
And the lame walk.
And He died for the sins
Of the whole world -
For mine and for yours.

This Friend was crucified -
Hanged upon a wooden Cross,
And left to die.
But death was not the end,
And He was raised
To life again - Lord of all.

Jesus Christ is His name,
And He longs to be
A special Friend to all
Who turn to Him in faith
And give their lives to Him.
For He is perfect Love.

Come to Him, then;
And He will be your Friend.
Although He lives
In inaccessible light,
He can dwell in your heart,
And give you eternal life.

Robert D Hayward

Second-Hand You

I'm stuck with the second-hand you
When I bought you, you were beautiful
But now you've turned to hate
I want my money back before it's too late
I still have the guarantee
I want my money back
Because love is free
You hate the sight of me
I was sold on a memory
But memories don't guarantee
A future that is happy
I'm scared there will be no return
For all the receipts you've burned
I'm stuck with you
Stuck with me
Only I can make myself happy
I'm stuck with the second-hand you.
I bought something beautiful
But love was always free.

Daniel White

My Friend Jean

I have a friend I met at work
Many years ago
The sort of friend, through thick and thin,
Is always good to know.
Retired now our lives have changed
And though many miles apart
We meet up sometimes when we can
And have a 'heart to heart'.
We moan a bit, then have a laugh
When we go out on a spree,
Then we set the world to rights
Over a scone and cup of tea.
Though mad or sad, through good and bad
We seem to muddle through
When we're flummoxed we have a chat
And work out what to do.
When tough times came I needed help
So my friend came on the scene
From many miles, to lend a hand
That is, my friend Jean.
Not once, nor twice, but ten times more
She journeyed to help me out
Her time so generously given
That's really caring, without a doubt.
My tribute to her is this small ode
To thank her for being there
When I needed a friend -
It was Jean who came
And showed me there's always
Someone special like her who'll care.

Mollie D Earl

For The Duration . . .

You Called The Other Day

You called, the other day, at the school parking space,
By your scooter, you said, under the tall blackboard trees
When the sun played with those leafy tresses;
I wasn't there to witness.

Some teacher brought it up, to you, with my drifting life,
A mystic story arousing your memories, added you,
When the orchid trees bloomed above the school fountain;
I wasn't there to see

The new library spark in daylight to accompany your steps
When you hurry from your old office desk to your class
Where the Chinese verses of old tangle before your glasses
To merge with the innocent eyes of the youths,

The bell chime eight times on and off a class the usual way
When the shadow of your long pacing legs, books in one arm
And the other waving hand with a few pens blue or red
Wafts even lonelier in the laughter of the students,

The buildings connected by corridors among banyan trees
With the aerial roots knotted like the ropes of scout boys
Where we used to debate upon the grandeur of poetry
When sparrows chirped to cheer with our speeches.

Time was short and the bell would chime again, you said,
But I could see your lonely shadow expand by my sight,
As if a day when your voice dimmed on my departure -
Holding on a dream to discover a voice of my own,

So, before you had to go for next class, I said, I was fine,
And all I did was to delineate with a most instinctive touch
The world under our glowing sun, then I wished you well,
While you sighed at once like night took over the light;

I wasn't there to watch before you hung up,
But the darkness leaked slowly into my heart.

David Lin

Brenna

We always said
You'd be the first one
To catch the train.
I tried to let it rain
When I heard,
But my mind preferred to wonder
Under cloudy skies,
Why?

Always balls-out,
Never one to shout,
'Saltwater' was our catchphrase
From sunnier days
By the light
Near the sea,
You and me.

You always were an oddball,
Stout
And tall
And fearless!
Ginger-topped
With eyes so blue,
You goon.
I'll never forget you.

Brett Goose RIP my friend.

Daniel Beale

Remembering Friends

I was trapped in a dark and gloomy place
Nowhere to turn, nowhere to go
Meeting you brought joy to my face
Stopped me feeling ever so low

Your words were always so kind
Knowing I had no confidence in life
There were ties of friendship which bind
When my world was full of strife

Fame and fortune now beckon you
No room for me who has a tiny part
I wish you well in everything you do
A friend who holds a special place in my heart.

Catriona

My Friend Freda

My friend Freda died today,
Nay she was more than a friend,
She was my adopted mother.
Freda is now at peace,
Reunited with her loved ones,
Her end was Peace,
May She Rest in that Peace
And Rise in Glory.

Janet Cavill

Creativity

Creativity is designing,
Shapes and colours to create forms,
Materials and technology for texture,
Different styles enhance function,
Whilst creating something new.

Creativity is composing
Notes and beats to create music,
Words and language for expressionism,
Genre gems evoke emotion,
Whilst creating something new.

Creativity is evolving,
Scents and perfumes to create moods,
Ingredients and methods for recipes
Varying trends spice up fashion,
Whilst creating something new.

Yeside Ogunkoya

Friendship

It was a vision of happiness
Now a vision in the drowsy gloom
Too many tears lovers shed
Many times our hearts break
In many doleful stories we see
The little sweet kills much bitterness
What once was tenderness
The richest juice to passion flowers grew
Now dead in poison flowers wilted
Twin roses by the winds blown apart
Only to meet more closely
And share each other's hearts.

Linda Bevan

Untitled

You knew where you were going
Why didn't you walk on by?
I could have lived without you,
But not without a sigh.

The months we had together
I ignored the shadows in my mind
Our love would be forever
Until the end of time.

I thought I had a future
And was happy and content
But there were no tomorrows
Your destiny was spent.

I didn't need this broken heart
Or the weight of sorrow
When the call came from Heaven
To end your stay on Earth.

Doreen Furmston

Cleo

The time it came for us to part
And when it did it broke our heart
But because we loved you so
We knew it was time to let you go
Now you are free from all pain
Once more can run and play again
Up above in that big blue sky
Your spirit did soar now you can fly
We know you'll have made lots of new friends
So to our Cleo all our love we do send.

Theresa Ann Sanderson

Anglesea

Groaning, heaving upwards from their ancient submergence
Vast plates crash into light, sucking air, throwing off desert seas
In a surge reel back stunned, from torn edges of land
Vast cliffs punch upwards, Cambrian fury slicing white cloud
In turn rent green and forests spring as dark as the pungent earth
That bore them, race down to the eternal conflagration
Crowd the froth and anger of the returning floods, clawing back
Mindless sediment once still - silence now roars above
Granite walls and parapets clinging to its tenuous foothold
And locking roots downward into the molten core welding
Solid the towering faces unmoveable gaze down in triumph
The tides receded sulking lapping quietly then, biding time
Planning, watching crept back and forth and creeps
Back and forth considering the quiet inevitabilities
Of eternity to erode and roll in mineral grinding
Smothering again, chancing to snatch particles, air and light
From fragile borders of resolve where rock and water
Quiver together in an uncomfortable equation.

Eternity, time enough for seas to crash and split
The flawed geology, ravage and flatten every visible stone
Pulverise land edges to sand, countered with spewing magma
Pushing battalions of spires outwards to fall and rebuild
Furious balance and futile struggles in barren borders
Gutted shell case and polished bones drift and roll
Sightless scavengers forage in endless graveyards
Turning over remains of the innocent and inadvertent
Sway in grim silence, mute and impartial
Witness to the conflict that rages in the coves and shores.

For The Duration . . .

The patterns and rhythms older than time's constant
Drumming incessant waves beneath the illuminated shores
Break on the sheltering headlands either side, rumble on
The purple heather, reverberating through bodies of the living
On seamless sky and sea and folded rock, shattered, salt-bleached
Denigration singing back to the cries of tern and shearwater
The gull's sly scream echoes out into pitiless horizons
Or downwards onto the indifferent backs of crab and mollusc
That clatter and cling, shivering in the chaos borders waiting
With infinite patience, for an end to the battle that has raged
And rages still quietly through the centuries.

I came here once millions of years later
With my daughter, she was three.
We walked in warm and liquid April sunlight and I watched
As she danced and tasted the water's edge all along
The lovely shifting plainness of the sea which swept away
To a luminous horizon as blue as her eyes that whirled
And dared me to charge along the edges with her
The colours blurred sky lit eyes and sky horizon
Until I looked right through her and could not see
Sky-lit eyes that for a moment had shot through me
Glimpsed a time long gone, standing motionless I gazed.

Younger coastline of silver and blue under a translucent sun
Scent of ancient wooded breezes, fragrant with pine
Blew along the shore and carried with it sounds
Of stones rattling into water and a surge and pull
Of insistent tides that glided and swirled
In ecstatic symmetries that swallow river silt and streams
Glacial wind, on shore that had been out at sea
For centuries, screaming and pushing white-topped waves
The chill of ice caps blowing through me, scalpel-sharp
Cutting out all sounds and feeling but faintly I sensed
Distant voices of creatures that had no place here.

Which jolted me millions years forwards and back
To the sparkling pools of her eyes that questioned
Why I wouldn't come into the water?
We raced along the shoreline edge belonging
Neither to the land or the sea but for a moment listened
Heard the wind's singing splashed in the margins
As elemental as the rumbling world around us
And took our place in its aeons of history.

Jeff Dipple

Secret Love

Your eyes are as the twinkling stars
    Upon a clear, dark, frosty night.
Your lips two rose petals are
    That languor in the morning light.
Your smile is as the streaming sun
    Emerging from a shroud of cloud,
The warmth and sweetness of its ray
    The angels have endowed.

My love for you grows stronger still
    With every hour, each passing day.
I would to tell you of its might,
    But cannot find the words to say.
So, deep within this heart of mine,
    My love, a prisoner, lies.
And must remain a captive there
    Until my body dies.

Charles Harvey

My Dear Friend And I
(For Sheilagh)

We would meet at Oxford railway station
every second month on a Saturday morning
She from Reading, I from Worcester.
Her smiling face always there to find me in the crowd.

We eagerly talked our way
up the long road to the town,
stopping to look in windows
of shops but never buying.
We made a beeline
for the antique market
studying the goods on the stalls,
and shared knowing comments.
In early years buying small guilt presents
for our children left at home.
Later spending the money on ourselves.
At Oxford market she bought
a tortoise she called Jude
and carried it home in a box.
Over the years we lunched in various cafés
as some closed and others opened.
We planned dream holidays together and never went.
In later life joyfully looking for scenes shot
from 'Inspector Morse' which we both loved.

A whole day together seemed long
but grew shorter as the years passed.
A brief escape from our faded lives,
not unhappy, not happy.

Now my dear friend and I
will never meet again
at Oxford railway station.

Helen Dalgleish

Sligo

I have taken a trip to Sligo
In the dear old Emerald Land
Its lakes and its mountains
And its scenery so grand

As I take a stroll along the road
To see the lovely lough gill
And Tobernalt not far away
The scene is so tranquil

An old churchyard comes into view
Where Yeats is laid to rest
And his father often preached the word
In the church he loved the best.
Benbulben too we must not forget
With its legend of other days
Its towering peak and stone so sleek
Looking out on the Atlantic waves

And as I go to see Glen Carr
With its waterfall flowing free
I stop and gaze at this lovely sight
On its journey to the sea.

I love to visit this lovely spot
Fond memories it holds for me
Going back to my childhood days
When I was young and free

And when I am old and weary
And my life has run is spell
I hope someone will lay me down
In the place I love so well.

B McGrath

Strangely, After All The Years . . .

You said you loved me
In the greyness of our years
You said you loved me . . . and
Strangely, I find myself profoundly sad.

Of course, within my head,
Far-off bells clang tinkling
As dreams and phantom memory
Drag kicking, into now.

You said you loved me
In the greyness of our years
You said you loved me . . . and
Strangely, my draining fear is absolute.

Why sad . . . ?
Sad for the lifetime of living
Swamped in the clay toil of being
Gone in the twinkling of a failing eye,
Time, not wasted, but lost.

And fear . . . why fear?
Fear from forgotten maiden days
And hugely component of love
Truncated now, in every fussy detail . . .
Afraid of fear, always the exquisite bar.

But the words are said . . .
In the greyness of our years
You said you loved me.
And therefore, we can bounce
And jump and dance and spin
And fly together into a setting haze of trust
As long as you will hold me by the hand.
Because of course, in simple terms . . . and
Strangely, after all the years, I love you still.

Jane Brooks

Soldier Boy

Oh I did love a 'Soldier Boy',
He was young and fair,
Azure blue his smiling eyes,
Sun-flecked gold his hair.
He loved me in such gentle ways,
With tender words and true,
Oh how I loved my 'Soldier Boy',
Though in my heart I knew
War's savage hand would beckon him
To heed his country's call,
In battle's strife
To give his life,
My tears in sorrow fall.
Time the 'healer' soothed the pain
Of grief-scarred anguished days;
Now in the twilight of my years
Sweet remembrance stays
Of one so young and fair -
Azure blue his smiling eyes,
Sun-flecked gold his hair,
As we remember all of those
Who died to keep us free,
I think of my dear 'Soldier Boy'
Who gave his heart to me.

Beryl Andrews

What's In A Name? - Angela

Angela, sweet Angela, the vision of my
Night-time dreams - how much do I adore thee.
God, what would I give to be lying there beside you dear, and
Even though we lay apart, split by miles,
Life is still so kind to me
As I contemplate our coming tryst.

To me you are my very breath;
Here I sit and fantasise and write as in a daze, but
Only when I feel your touch does
My heart and body come alive -
Angela, my sweet, delightful own; the object of my
Sweet and lovely muse - how much do I adore thee?

Alan Whitworth

Lust Not Love

Could you, would you, risk it
All for just one moment of time?
One moment of madness,
Caught up in the flames of desire.
Caught up in lies,
If only for one night.
An all or nothing feeling
Fuelled by our lies.

Pamela McCormack

Marriage

They say you hurt the one you love
But what does it achieve?
We scream and bawl and rant and rave
And then you pack to leave.
But we know we love each other
And for me there'll be no other.
Yet we cannot seem to reach that peak of peace divine.
I seem to bring about the worst
It's as though we're Devil cursed.
Must we carry on until we blow our mind?

The ache in my heart is telling me
A life apart could never be
Yet I hurt you bad and cannot stand the pain
You're almost to the door and my heart begins to pour
And I'm begging you to please come back again
What on earth shall I do
I know I'll be the death of you
I'd cut my heart and tongue out if I could
That hurt look on your face it's driving me insane
For when I hurt you it's my heart that weeps its blood

I can make all the promises that you want to hear
But darling I'd say anything, just to keep you near.
'I'll cook your meals. I'll clean your house
I'll be as quiet as a mouse . . . only sweetie, please turn around
Honey don't walk out the door, I'll be good and that's for sure
Come back to my arms let me feel your magic charms
I'll never say another thing that shoots you to the ground.

I can be so awfully sweet
Devour you like a treat
Put you in a paradise from which you won't awake
Ah, but I can see you're bent on leavin'
Well just see who does the grievin'
As far as I'm concerned
You can go jump in the lake.

Celia Caroline Layton

For The Duration . . .

As If

As if, a rose
could express my love
For you
I behold
For you
I would die

As if, the sky
was blue enough
For you
It's yours
For you
To behold

As if, my heart
was big enough
For you
Take it
For you,
It's yours
Treasure it

As if, my life
was long enough
For you to share
For you to care
Savour it
Just you

As if, my soul
was deep enough
For you to sail
Eternity's journey
For you
For now
For ever
It's yours.

Ivana Cullup

House Of Stone

We thought we would build a house
As children we wanted a den
We decided to build it in a tree
We were only the age of ten

I climbed up high upon a branch
And my brother stood down below
He started passing stones to me
But the building was very slow

All was going well for a while
The house was three stone high
Then a mistake, I dropped one
On my brother, he began to cry

My mother came out in a hurry
And how she scolded me
For being so very stupid
Building a house of stone in a tree.

Catherine Armstrong

Sweet Words

These sweet words,
For my sweet love,
From myself are
Never enough.

Colin Hush

Sleep Soft

Sleep soft, sweet nymph, by Eastern breezes lulled
In freshening rest and undisturbed repose;
With gentle sleep be all thy senses dulled,
Sleep soft, as first dew sleeps upon the rose.
May tender angels minister to thee,
Guarding thy slumbers from all outward harm,
Heal all thy troubles, from all cares set free
And to thy holy mind give inmost calm.
Sleep soft, pure virgin, and amid thy rest
May this most precious gift be also thine:
That sweetest dreams of all thou lovest best
May give delight unto thy closed eyes.
May such rare pleasures thine this night-time be:
Sleep soft, sweet nymph, sleep soft, and dream of me.

Rev Barrie Williams

For My Friend

I appreciate your love, gentleness
And kindness
Always available and ready to help
Me out of a mess
Your thoughtfulness is just unreal
Thank God you're not like some, as fickle onion peel!
You are uncomplicated without the many layers
Of those I've often met who turned out to be players.
So thank you dear Fay for who you are
You are truly one of my best friends
By far.

Joy Elaine Mendez

Just My Valentine

It seems like only yesterday,
You were my *Valentine*
We kissed and cuddled in the park - you vowed you would be mine.
You were so strong and handsome then, and I a maiden shy,
But we knew our lives would soon be joined -
And how those years did fly.
You're not so young or handsome now,
In fact you're bald and tubby,
But you're still my only *Valentine*
My kind and thoughtful hubby!
And though you're now a grandad,
And I am grandmother,
We've got what no else has - *we've still got each other!*
Happy Valentine's Day.

Enid Crowhurst

Your . . .

Your name is written upon my heart
Your words are spoken in my ear
Your love it does softly kiss my lips
Your eyes have penetrated my soul
Your touch aroused my silent senses
Your smile lights up my darkness
You flesh excites my wildest dreams
Your passions let my spirit soar
Your desires encapsulate my world
Your name is the woman I love.

Simon Cook

My Fuel

After that fling, I realised I need you more,
I stopped drinking, no weed, no more,
I wormed my way back to you,
I had to, I'm not mad at you,
You reminded me, why I was attracted to you,
I know I acted the fool, acted cruel,
But I didn't pack the tool, blast the fool,
I'm tactful, girl! - you make me drool,
You're my fuel, we truly love each other,
Together we can teach each other,
Under the covers you know how to pleasure me,
Kiss and caress me, ecstasy,
You lift me up when I'm feeling down,
You've got me dancing on the ceiling now,
No more frown, my problems you solve them,
You were right not to involve them.

James Hazell

Rebecca

You must have known you'd be breaking my heart
When you laid with a lad you did not love
For your wild, careless fling there's a price
For now we wait but not with joy
For one small blameless soul
Unwanted and as yet unloved
To join a broken home.
It will be hard, you'll have to work
While crèche and minders take your place
No love at home to mop tired tears and share the load
To answer endless questions 'Where's my dad?'
It's then you know you are alone.

Judy McEwan

First Of Many
(Written for my father died 11 04 2008)

Time to reflect
Best keep the light on
Only way
To see a Star

Daddy was a Star
To me still is
The night sky
Full of bright stars

What stories I have
To brighten my past year
Only missing
My real Star

Honesty and integrity
Two years of a Star
Both burn bright
Throughout the night

God keep you safe
My bright Star
Guide men
From afar.

An anniversary
Not a sermon
A reflection
First of many.

Anton Nicholas

First Kiss Blues

Oh, the beauty of that sunny day!
How wonderful just to be with you!
A short and sweet picnic in the park.
Not a care in the world.
There you were, stunning yet serene.
I reach forward to touch your hand.
You caressed my cheek.
I wanted to kiss you then.
A silent sigh swept over me.
I rested my head on the grass.
We looked up at the clouds together.
Two clouds coasted across the sky.
'Do you think they're in love, too?'
We made our way across town.
The streets as busy as they ever were.
'I've got to go to classes!' you said . . .
And suddenly it happened . . .
You kissed me, instinctively.
I kissed you back, longingly.
It was so sudden, almost perfect . . .
With a bit of planning, it could have been.
But that first kiss only happens once. . .
In a second it was done,
Never to be repeated.
Yet with it comes, the hope for seconds . . .
'See you tomorrow!' you said . . .
Leaving me to live
The loneliest day of my life
Without you . . .

Denis Martindale

Thailand -
The Land Of A Thousand Smiles

Thais give customary weis, ladies are presents with leys;
Visit life size and larger golden Buddha statues;
Or maybe try an adventure on a wonderful Siamese sea-cruise!
Caves converted into temples and shrines;
For many a monk and nun to study the divine;
You can trek into the heart of the jungle
Go riding on an elephant in the Golden Triangle!
There are rubber plantations there; where monkeys and raccoons play.
Tuc-tuc rides for a few thrills; and lady-men for the gay!
Natural hot water springs are great for you to relax in;
Although you shouldn't miss a trek across the mountains;
When the moon is waxing!
You can visit mysterious hill-tribes
For totally different kinds of vibes!
Eat fresh coconut, stay in a bamboo hut;
Relax on a palm-fringed beach;
With a Singha beer within reach!
Visit Tet for a tête à tête
With the world as your oyster, you can travel for miles
- You might as well go to the Land of a Thousand Smiles!

Colette Breeze

Holding Hands
(In remembrance of my dear wife 'Betty' September 7th 2006)

When you have lost someone to you so very dear,
Do not be afraid to show your sorrow and shed that extra tear,
For having been together for so many years,
Behind all the laughter now, there will always be the tears.

There will be so many hours and days with time to kill,
And this will take its toll, even on the strongest will.
No more can you turn around and see the face you love,
She has gone to rest in the arms and care of God above.

So now you must try to fill your days with things to do,
And find strength in knowing that she loved you too.
Hold out your hand, and God will always lead the way,
To comfort and guide you, into the future, and through every day.

Albert Bennett

Kelly

When snowdrops and crocus were new on the lawn,
This was the time little Kelly was born,
Her beautiful features right down to her toes
Those tiny wee fingers which held one of ours
Like the new flower petals so fragile and small
Our precious new daughter was smaller than all.

But all springtime flowers so short is their lot,
The beauty they give us will ne'er be forgot.
Now she's tended by angels way up there so far,
So look up, you'll see her, our own little star.

Julie Haggis

Too Young To Be A Man

A man to my mother
Can't be a child
The true feeling I have to hide
My life is incomplete without my dad
Birthday and Christmas cards, his name disappears
A letter from school
Addressed to Mrs not Mr
I mss my dad's laugh
Especially his jokes
The risen voice when I am in trouble
The special sweets he bought
Dad trying to unstick his from his false teeth
The stories of his youth
My dad always believed in the truth
I miss football
I miss the little toys he hid in his coat for me
Parks and nature centre he took me
Our house is empty without Dad
I am angry and mad
But for my mother
I try to hide my feeling
Too young to be a man
Too young to understand.

Kim Gourlay Almey

The Cousins

We are cousins with the same surname
We were born the same month, same year
In school, alphabetically we're sat on the same desk
We had also the same kind of intelligence
Her mother was a strict headmistress
Mine was at home disabled and loving
We finished our primary school
With the same grades
Nelly-Jean was sent to university
I just carried on at the same college
Not far from home
To be qualified 'Perfect young Lady'
I was taught to cook, wash and sew
I didn't like it but I had to care for my mum
My cousin quickly obtained her BA in maths
I went in Congo - Africa
It was a small village in middle of the jungle
I needed washing, cooking and sewing for survival
We are now both in our autumn years
My cousin never moved from home, divorced twice
My life was full of surprises and love
I was the poorest but the privileged one.

Victorine Lejeune-Stubbs

Last In Line

How I hated PE lessons at school,
I always felt like such a fool!
When they picked teams, I'd be last in line,
In no kind of sports did I ever shine.

My sportier classmates viewed me with disgust,
Nobody wanted to take me but they knew they must;
They'd have preferred to leave me standing there,
If they hurt my feelings, they didn't really care.

I never enjoyed hockey a single bit,
Tried to dodge the sticks in case I was hit;
The opposing team cheered when I was told one day
To be the goalkeeper, knowing that the match would go their way.

Netball was the same - I was just as useless,
Each second of those matches dragged, I must confess;
I'd inevitably misjudge every throw,
Passing the ball to the other team, so their score would grow.

In tennis, I could never hit the ball over the net,
It was sure to end up in the stream, on that you could bet!
I'd spend most of the lesson fishing it out
And vividly recall how my teacher would shout.

Only once did I make them eat each word,
A single success on me was conferred;
Thanks to a skipping tournament, this came about,
If you tripped over the rope, you were out.

I was the last one left standing that afternoon,
The hours I'd spent skipping as a child were a real boon;
I still remember their faces filled with surprise,
As if they couldn't believe their eyes!

Annabelle Tipper

Sitting In A Field In The Sun

I remember the days of school
As being pretty cool
The teachers were very nice
Always there to give advice
School dinners always treat
Made of real meat
Mashed potatoes by the ton
Enough vegetables to make you run
With gypsy tart and spotty dick
Covered with custard that was so thick
Ate so much - it made me sick
Semolina was something I hated
And needed to be sedated
Despite the dollops of jam
I still preferred roast lamb
I remember those good old days
And the terrible school plays

The country run where I collapsed
Too much sun and not enough fun
The hurdles, the high jump and the rest
Was something I liked best
Who came first
Was always a real contest
The 100 metres - I came first
That really was the very best
I remember those days of fun
Sitting in a field in the sun
Hearing the teacher blow his whistle
Ready for our dismissal.

Simone Farrugia Meiszner

Sixty Years Of Trying

Did I like my schooldays?
Yes, I did in part
But I wasn't very smart
I found reading quite hard going
Hoped my friends were not too knowing
But they were and helped me some
The sweetie jar never came my way
And so I just went on out to play.

On Friday my friend took me home to tea
From pavement cracks we would always flee
From the shop on the corner
We bought some sweets
Friday was the day for treats

When we sat the Eleven Plus
My friend she passed
But I did not
But then we moved
And it did not matter
To me my new school was much better
I loved the cooking and the sport
I think I was quite well taught

Later to the Convent I travelled on a bus
Wearing a second-hand uniform
But I didn't make a fuss
I won a ribbon for walking tall
I won a cup for singing an' all

Yes I learned to read and write
Yes I grew and gained much height
With perseverance I passed my test
I went to college and did my best
Now I help the children who
Just like me find it hard to spell
But with much hard work
Learn to do quite well.

Barbara Tozer

My Old Friend Pete

As I walked along the street
I met my old friend Pete
He said, 'Let's go to a bar
And have a jar.'
I said, 'That's a good idea
I don't half fancy a beer.'
We had a good blether
Mostly about the weather
He said, 'This is great
But I can't stay too late.'
I said, 'Have one before you go'
He said, 'You're a good guy to know.'
Then we went on our way
The end of a great day.

Frank Tonner

Friendship

If ever you should feel you're on your own
Have reached the end, and simply can't go on
If ever you can't face another day
Or solve a problem - find another way
Then think of me, I'm always somewhere near
And we will find an answer - never fear
Just think, *how would I act? What would I do?*
So though I may not always be with you
You'll find the answer, where you thought was none
You see - I leave myself in you although I may be gone
Just face life's problems bravely, as they come
Do not despair - my heart is in your home.

Gordon Andrews

The Fastest Gun Alive

He strutted round the schoolyard,
Bogus pistols by his side.
Throwing down his challenge,
Leaving us no place to hide.

'Slap leather,' he would holler,
Catching us off guard.
His cold eyes clearly focused,
His lips set firm and hard.

Some called him relentless,
Others thought him manic.
Many of us 'bit the dust',
The rest ran off in panic.

One day I turned the tables
And caught him by surprise.
He stared at me quite blankly,
Fear flashing through his eyes.

'Draw your doggone varmint,'
I shouted in his face.
Then pulled my 'guns' out quickly,
While his stayed in their place

He seemed so disconcerted,
Then began to sob and sigh.
A distant look was on his face,
A teardrop in his eye.

His behaviour seemed surprising,
As cowboys never cried.
It was nearly three days later,
When I learned his mum had died.

Paul Kelly

Homework

What it is to remember the days of homework
When all was what had been done last night
Or not done
When the great fear
Of what had happened
Homework forgotten
And excuses, excuses
The dog ate it
The cat ate it
Sheep ate it, goats ate it
Everything in creation ate it
It fell out of my bag
It got thrown away
It was used as toilet paper
By mistake
By all and sundry
It fell out of the car
It fell in a puddle
It fell in the fire
It fell everywhere it could
It was too hard
There was too much of it
I couldn't do it all
I was sick
Sick of the homework
Sick of having to do it
Sick of this intrusion in my free time
When all should be play and fun
After days of clock and bell.

Alasdair Sclater

For Our Old Love When

When Audrey, Natalie and fair Julie too,
Were as real then to me as I knew I was to you,
We'd leave our dark theatre often only to find
Wet sidewalks and streets by rain cleanly defined,
With welcome night air so soft, easily breathed,
We sensed our lives one, sum of all we believed.

Hurrying home surely seemed outside of reason.
Holding and touching were always in season.
Holly-red winters, rosy white, dogwood springs,
Heady gardenia summers, autumn mums' strings,
Held us charmed by sweet, sight-scented delights,
Hypnotically entranced in cool, silky soft nights.

Even rare moments when we were sometimes apart,
Evening dreams' trains or dewdrop mornings' start,
Echoed with sighs, sweet sighs to you and me,
Erecting bridges that met across obstacles and sea,
Ever held magically by love's brawn and blood,
Even when bridges collapsed, cleaving us by the flood.

Now, sometimes you phone, you made that your choice,
Never letting me leave one soft sound in your voice,
Nearly same soft sound as your voice I remember,
Nor letting my eyes see you in our now grey December.
Nightly wet, rain-washed streets I tenderly then recall
Naked, new, in Eden once more, our time before the fall.

Edgar Wyatt Stephens

Reaching Out

There in the photographs
You smile back at me.
What a lovely time we had
That day down by the sea.
And there you are once again,
Christmas decorations everywhere.
That Christmas was so special,
We didn't have a care.
Autumn leaves were falling
Forming a carpet on the ground
The smile on your face says it all
As you gaze at the beauty around.
Happy Birthday . . . it came again
Surrounded by presents . . . you smile.
Smiling was something that you did well
How it brightened every mile.
I don't have you anymore
Your life has slipped away
But your smile reaches out from photographs
And wipes my tears away.

Joyce Hudspith

Friends

We go back such a long, long way
Teenage friends at school
Always right, the future bright
We thought we knew it all.

Rather spoilt and pampered
The biggest plan to make
Was what to wear on Saturday
And which handbag should we take.

Fifty years on, how time has flown
Did we ever reach that goal?
Many fears and sometimes tears
But we got there on the whole.

Busy, busy, busy
With barely time to rest
But the house seems quiet and lonely
Now the brood have flown the nest.

The road was sometimes bumpy
With its many twists and bends
But we were always there for each other
And we're still the best of friends.

Sheelah Collier-Ringer

Big Sister

My sister is fantastic - she's clever and frightfully nice.
She's friendly and charming
And very disarming
And dishes out good, sound advice.

Her patience is commendable, her wittiness quite keen;
Her attitude, when under stress, remarkably serene.
She's capable and competent; in fact it's safe to say
She's pretty much an icon in each and every way.

We're both grown up now and she's overseas,
But she's still a tower of strength
With her kind words of sympathy,
She's always there for me;
I could ramble on at great length!

Suffice it to say
That there isn't a day
Goes by when I don't think of what
A wonderful person
She is, that is certain;
She's everything that I am not!

Heather Pickering

My Sister, My Friend

I need not tell her how I feel she knows.
She shares my tears of joy as children grow.
And gives me strength as they walk hand in hand
To make their way as we have done.
She shares my grief when anxious times prevail
And holds me fast when parents say goodbye.

Benevolent friend, your applause of voice says it all
When times are blessed with gain or self acclaim.
Impartial observer, you accept my account of truth
And assure me by you removing doubt.
I need not conform to expectation nor do battle with words
But express at will while fearing no retribution.

My sister, my friend, you are my rock, your friendship is my gold
That shines with warmth and unbiased love.
And as our time draws nigh a tighter hold prevails
Too soon just yet to think our bond will break.
And yet I know we will unite above and share our everlasting love
And meet again with kin we loved so dear
Who made it all worthwhile.

Joan Hosker

Thank You
(Dedicated to remembering friends at Emmanuel Church, Sidcup, Kent)

Remembering you, loyal and true,
still keeping in touch as you do;
it makes each week worthwhile to seek
and enjoy all things here I find new,
for knowing you're there, dear friends to share
all the news whether sad, dull or fair,
brings me your smiles across all the miles,
knowing you're special and care.

Thanks for the sharing, the years of caring,
the welcomes and 'How are you faring?'
it has meant so much that you've kept in touch
and listened to all my daring!
I remember each day the 'Emmanual way'
of linking our friendships, and pray
that through all our years of gladness and tears
in Christ we're together each day.

Thank you, dear friends, and God bless you all.

Ann Voaden

My Best Friend

J ade is a true friend
A lways there to defend
D oing all she can for me
E very day she is all she can be

L ovely ginger hair which is pretty
O ut for a day shopping in the city
U nderstand my problems and helps me through
I ntelligent and kind and does all she can do
S eeing sense through thick and thin
E verything she does comes with no sin

S he is my best friend
A nd I hope our friendship never ends
I don't want to lose her at all
N othing can penetrate our friendship, not even the strongest wall
T hank you Jade for being my best friend.

Rosie Hinwood

Miss Tammy Buckner

Miss Tammy Buckner,
She is encouraging me!
She thinks I can write!
I have confidence!
I can believe in myself
Because of Tammy!
She loaned me a book!
It is 'For The Writer's Soul'!
She's my cheerleader!

Laraine Smith

For The Duration . . .

Transience

Life is for living
Death is never far away.
Love is for giving
In each and every day.

Make the most of all our hours,
One day the clock will stop.
Enjoy the fields, smell the flowers,
Before their petals drop.

As the years proceed inexorably on,
Ever faster with our increasing ages
Yesterday, today, tomorrow will have gone,
A novel with its all too finite pages.

When this game of life is nearly past
We can look back on the years all spent,
Constant to our loved ones till the last
And we will know; our time was well meant.

John Willmott

Like A Twin

We share our secrets and together laugh and shout,
There is lots of noise when we are out and about.
Known for the practical jokes we play a-plenty,
Once convinced neighbour I was buying a Bentley.

Going on holiday every year is a joy,
Egg each other on to find ourselves a toy boy.
'Grow up,' say others, 'You're supposed to be mature.'
We reply, 'Don't be silly, that would be a bore.'

You are like the twin sister I have never had,
Like me you're brown-haired, blue-eyed and equally mad.
United, our ambitions we mainly fulfil,
Without you my life would be unbearable.

Susan Mullinger

Friendship

(This poem is dedicated to Julie and Joanna for being the perfect friends)

Friendship is a wonderful thing
To have
We value each other when times
Are rough
A friend is always there to lend
A helping hand
When you're feeling down
Our friendship grows like a rose
And when we are not together
We are never far apart
I learnt the value of our wonderful friendship
Because it is timeless and everlasting
In each and every day.

Our friendship has grown through the years
It cannot be faltered or bought
As it comes from the heart with love
I have learnt the value of having a good
Friend in you
Because our friendship is always here to
Stay in each other's hearts.

The time we shared together is priceless
As we embrace the joys of life
From laughter to our sorrows
It is everlasting as we are always
There to care about each other and watch
Out for one another like good friends do
For this is what being friends is all about.
It is always true and very loyal

If only I can keep it bottled up
For many years
What we have and to share with the rest of the world
They would see how true our friendship is
Because having such a wonderful friend
Is just like having sisters to share the same interests
And a talk about things that I could not tell
Anyone else about

As I share your kindness with love and affection
That having you both around makes my
World seem brighter
I learnt the value of our friendship
As we laugh and cry
It is a ray of sun on a cloudy day.

I learnt to value your friendship
Because you fulfil my life
With such wonderful things
That friends could bring
Just having dearest friends like you.

Samantha Rose Whitworth

Farewell To A Friend
(For Moha Sani Hassan)

I am joyously sad
My dear friend
As your dreams are fulfilled
New paths we must lead
As our destinies become untwined
I am happy your dreams are come true
Yet sad it keeps us apart
We are close but far
For the bond our two hearts share
Distance cannot break
Even if you live so far away
Our love will not wither
Here I stand laughing in tears
As I wave you goodbye
Our friendship will stay alive
But in a new form and way
Is in indeed a bittersweet moment
As our past becomes history
And our future presents a brand new page.

Debra Ayis

Four Seasons: Poem For Uncle Eric

So you've shed your skin and gone away
To a place where the sky is never grey.
Without you it won't be the same
For the rest of us, who here remain.

In a way, though, I'm glad that I
Didn't have the chance to say goodbye;
This way, I can always remember you
When your eyes sparkled brightly, like morning dew.

I'll think of you in the early spring
When life bursts into bloom and the birds start to sing,
When the cool air turns into a warmer breeze,
When I see the new buds on the plants and the trees.

When I walk by the sea in the midsummer rain,
I'll think of you and feel happy again.
I'll remember you by different shades of green
And the prettiest flowers that I've ever seen.

When the crisp autumn leaves fall down all around,
When their rainbow of shades covers up the ground,
I'll think of you fondly, stop for a while,
And as I catch the leaves, I'll smile.
When the strong winter sun shines through the trees,
When temperatures drop, and the ground starts to freeze.
I'll think of you when I walk by the sea,
Inhaling fresh air, feeling powerful and free.

When I see a small hill or a very high mountain,
Whenever I pass a large, flowing fountain,
When I smell the sea air, hear the trickle of a stream,
I'll think of you, living your brand new dream.

When I think of you I can't be sad
Because you're the best friend we've ever had.
So I'm letting you go, for I know that one day
Our souls will pass somewhere on life's motorway.

Melanie Ann Calvert

That's What Friends Are For

Someone to soothe your anger
When you want to scream and shout
Somebody who'll tell you it's okay
That's what friendship's all about.

Someone who'll keep you going
When a mountain greets your sight
Who'll help you work around it
And see that you're alright.

Somebody who will pick you up
When you're feeling down
Who will give you plenty of courage
When yours is on the ground.

Somebody who will talk to you
When you're feeling sad and blue
A friend who can make you laugh
And feel as good as new.

Donna Salisbury

My Tom Cat

My best friend is my cat
Who is getting really fat
As I feed him with fat
He hardly catches a rat
His name is Tom Jack Smith
And he's the stuff of myths
He's the one I'm always with
He's like a kin or kith
My cat Tom is my life
Looks like he's mine for life
Of course, he has nine lives
I feed him - he smiles and jives.

Muhammad Khurram Salim

Jenny It's You

When we were wed in sixty-two
We had not discussed
The possibility of children
Some form of contraception was a must.

Some six weeks past from being wed
Doctor saw me and said, 'Maybe
You've got an upset tum,
Or you're going to have a baby.'

We were living in a one room flat
And just starting married life
But we were happy and surprised
I was to be both Mum and wife.

Just two days over my due date
At five o'clock that July morn
Labour started, and at 2pm
My lovely girl was born.

How times have changed
For giving birth today
Can be made easy with an epidural
To take all that pain away.

We are proud of our lovely daughter
She's sensible and bright
She's best of friends with Dad and me
Helping hands for each other feels just right

She has worked hard to make her way
Not one to shirk a task
She now has her own family
What more could a mum ask?

She didn't do too well at school
But is always keen to learn
She studied hard for an extra year
To gain skills, for a good wage to earn.

Left with distinctions in her exams
Took her skills to join office life
Worked in various recruitment companies
Juggled being mother and wife

She will still take up new challenges
And studying for yet a higher grade
She is also a Magistrate
A successful life she's made.

You can tell how much we love her
And how proud we feel each day
She dearly loves her mum and dad
What more can her mum say?

Sheila Bates

Friendships Past

I sit and ponder as my mind goes back
To my many friends whom I have lost track
Over the years one makes many friends then we part
We go our own ways but they stay in one's heart
Where are they now? I often try to think
It would be nice to meet for a chat and a drink
The good times with friends I like to recall
When we were out on the town and having a ball
All the memories I retain, some of joy, some of pain
Like walking back home in a downpour of rain
I remember the tumbles and falls at the ice rink
The horrible tie you wore of shocking pink
If only we could go back and start over again
We are now all married and life is so tame.
I sit and ponder and my mind is not slack
I would love those carefree days back.

Leonard A G Butler

Sister-Friends

A sunny day in Victoria
On Vancouver Island,
The year was 1995
A special holiday for Ruth - and me.

We had strolled around the harbour
Taken a coach trip which was free
Then found the popular Delicatessen
And went in for a cup of tea.

She greeted us so warmly,
Our young waitress, and full of fun
Laughingly, she talked to us
Eager to hear our English tongue!

Now we are not exactly lookalikes
Except for our auburn hair;
Yes, we both are widows
Yes, we are good friends.

'How long have you known each other?'
'We've been friends for seventy years.'
'Seventy years! You're kidding!'
Said she in great bewilderment.

In puzzlement she looked at us
'Can't you guess whom we must be?
Ruth was born when I was two,
We're sisters, don't you see!'

Now in this Year 2009
We still love to tell the tale
Thankful that we still are sisters
And that friendship does not fail.

Agnes Hickling

St Paul's Church, Banbury

One of life's joys is family - where love is spread around
So, it's doubly nice to have 'two' of them - where fellowship abounds!
We meet each week here at St Paul's to show how much we
love our Lord
We sing His praise, and worship Him, all with one accord.
Amongst these kindred spirits, friendship fills the air
Long-lasting - as our saviour - someone there to care.
Although we're sometimes lonely, and sometimes we feel low
We always feel supported by the kind friends that we know.
Christ Jesus gave a promise 'to be with us to our end'
And as we travel our life's road 'St Paul's' is our best friend.

Edna Sparkes

Stuart

You would have walked here,
Spent time in peace,
At rest, communing within yourself,
Without,
With God and nature.
Clouds or rain,
Whatever fleeting worry charmed away by the
Welcome knowledge of family,
Home, friends.
Who, like a familiar gesture,
Are here to translate the essence
Of your life into
A more tangible substance we commemorate,
And in commemorating
You move amongst us.

Richard Muirhead

Thirty Years On

I heard the voice before the man
But higher, weaker than my mind
Remembered, across the span
Of many years; a sort of blind

Had closed our past away
Then unexpected hazard shone the light
Of recollection: I used to pay
Scant notice to the flight

Of years, but now, with balding pate
And feebler limbs I saw my friend
To whom a less kind fate
Had dealt the card of Parkinson

Tennis had he played, and all
The sports of youthful man:
A handsome man, and tall
And ne'er a thought for life's short span.

Now as he entered in the hall
His pace abated, head still high
But faltering as if to fall
I scarce concealed my sorrow's sigh.

We shared a brief heartfelt embrace
No English cool our greeting froze
And conversation went apace
We spoke of friends we'd known, and those

Who'd died; they were not few
For now mature, we them had passed
No pint their passing now to rue.
And so life's dice were blindly cast.

His eyes the same, a lambent hue
Direct and piercing windows of his mind
Which now despite enfeebled tongue
As high and sharp I still did find.

And as I listened to his croak
My mind began the sense to hear
And though at first distracted by the cloak

Of his infirmity I saw the sheer
Raw courage of the man: his every word
Betrayed the flame still burned within
And old respect once more was stirred -
I knew this man would always win.

Geoffrey Speechly

With Humble Hearts

Dear Lord, we lift our praise to You,
For the sun up in the sky,
The warm, but gentle, summer breeze,
And the white clouds drifting by.

We praise You for the lovely songs
Of the birds, both large and small,
For the beautiful flowers, the rippling grass,
And the trees, all standing tall.

We give our thanks for the many crops
All ripening in the fields,
Potatoes, carrots, peas and beans,
For *all* the bounteous yields.

Our hearts are full of wonder, Lord,
That for us, you've so much love,
For we are just such little specs
In the Universe above.

All through our lives, with humble hearts,
We'll give our thanks to You,
For You're our God, our faithful friend,
No matter what we do.

Lucy Williams

Tommy Willowbhy
(Dedicated to a childhood friend)

School had finished, and
The kids were glad,
And Tommy Willowbhy had
Been bad.

Low reports, for the
Year, his mother couldn't
Believe it, she shed a
Tear.

Hanging in a gang, and
Smoking cigarettes,
She always thought he'd
Join the cadets.

Truancy in the café on
The pinball machine,
She always thought he'd
Keep his character clean.

Going in the pub at
The age of fourteen,
Fighting in the cinema
During Steve McQueen.

Tommy Willowbhy was not
That bad, to have him
As a childhood friend
I was glad.

Francis Page

My Fanciful Friend

Like a spectre, you walk
Through dreams of
Deep believing senses.
I reach out and touch
Your soul, a borrowed
Fantasy.
Alive in my inner mind
You carry me
Through this
Physical world of non-existence.
Without you, I
Would not survive.
Close enough to touch. You
Remain in another dimension
Away from me
Away.

Lesley Glendinning

Friendship And Love

That summer of swaying grass
Nourished lasting friendship
Which turned to love
At winter's birth.

For thirty years - or more
Love brought joy
To a hungry heart
And when the hunger passed
Earth was covered
By falling snow.

Arthur Pickles

When We Were Young

Remember the nights we stayed out until dark
The songs we made up while we played in the park

Remember the names that we carved on the trees
And the free little gifts we got from the Chinese.

Remember defrosting baguettes in the dryer
And dipping some battered Mars bars in the fryer

Remember the tricks we played on your kid brother
And the constant attempts to try to fool your dear mother

Remember the day we met up after years
There was chatter and laughter and some happy tears
It was then that I knew we'd be friends till the end
For you are one person on whom I can depend!

Lisa Cresswell Wilkinson

Freda's Ministry Of Hugs

There's no one quite like Freda,
She is one heavenly gal,
Everyone totally loves her,
I'm so thrilled she's my pal!

She's a very special lady,
A prayer-warrior as well,
Her Bible ever at the ready,
To me, that's just swell!

So if you are in trouble,
Or overwhelmed with cares,
You just call on Freda,
She'll touch Heaven with her prayers.

If you are sad or lonely,
Join Freda's holy huddle,
You'll feel the love of Jesus,
When Freda gives you cuddles.

Laura Maxwell

Faraway Friend

My adult heart lurches
When thinking of my faraway friend
Saved by the child I was reminding
We'll be close till the end.
Yes borders and mountains apart us,
One is as close as one so chooses to be
For the present lasts but a moment
Your life as a whole is encased and lived in memory.
So I am remembering you now
A comfort in having you near
Loneliness is not a thing
Not a thing my faraway friend to fear.

Our every first conquest
Over the world beyond our doors
Our bogeyman, stingy nettles
Scabby-kneed wars.
Masters of the universe
Back gardens and beyond,
A river crossing to match Columbus
Curfews and school gates to abscond
Whole night skies to ponder,
Comic books to debate
Battle strategies to plan out
Ant colonies' fate
From fortifying a cabin
To a mortifying misconception,
An embarrassment turned tear-jerking laughter
Through a friend to friend connection.

The world is much vaster and less exciting
Than I believed back then
And in that very vastness that separates us
Our memories bring us together again.

Shelley Farr

My Special Friend

He remains my special friend
He taught me how to live
But most of all he taught me
Always to forgive
He said, 'Be kind to others
Then they will be kind to you'
So follow in his footsteps
Is what I have to do
When the angels took him
He knew how much I cried
In my grief I heard him saying
'I am still here by your side'
So I know forever
He watches over me
And each day from his photo
His smiling face I see
We still walk together
That is very plain
And one day in Heaven
I will meet my friend again.

Margaret Thompson

A Secret Illness

Powerless to help you
I see your worried face
Avoidance of the slightest touch
Lest germs should take their place

I see the water falling
Washing hand, tears cleansing eyes
Those that do not know you well
Cannot see through the disguise

A cruel and vicious cycle
Tiny links connect the chain
Let me be our anchor
Help your mind refrain

Panic holds you in its spell
Frustration shakes your bones
Stomach-turning, crippling dread
Imprison you at home

Tiny steps to freedom
Hand in hand we will begin
To fight the evil demons
Controlling from within.

Lynn Elizabeth Noone

Thoughts Of A Dying Friend

Below the thorntree of life
Belies timewarded betrayal of inner sanctity
Until the purification of love becomes salted with
Blissful intent of demons of the soul
The trees now glisten with disrespect
Tears of a thousand lovers of covet beauty
Until peace is found in the hidden gems
Of history's churches and sacred texts
Which seek escapism from earthly desires
And torment of the inner mind
Until all is reckless oblivion
In the subconscious state of alcoholism
With the memory dulled
By the shabby onset of reality
With the dawn awaking to all that is mundane
And beauty is fading fast.

Finnan Boyle

For My Sister And Friend

Our lives are so different in so many ways
And thousands of miles keep us apart
But no matter what life may throw at us
You will always have a special place in my heart.

Our sisterly bond can never be broken
It just grows stronger throughout the years
As does the love that we have for each other
Through all of the laughter and tears.

I think of you each and every day
Wishing we could spend more time together
But I am so grateful that you are my sister
And best friends we will stay forever.

Stella Mortazavi

Turning Three!

My cat, my tea,
It's all mine, it belongs to me.

My mum, my dad,
If you don't come now, I'll be bad.

I'll stamp my feet, I'll roll around,
Inside, outside, on the ground.

My teddy, my doll,
My funny, hairy, little troll.

I am three, I am three,
And everything belongs to me.

I can shout, and I can yell,
I'll find someone who I can tell . . .

. . . that 'I am three and can't you see,
That everything belongs to me?'

Now I'm nice, good and sweet,
I think I'm in for a little treat.

It's my birthday, couldn't be better,
Granny knitted me a sweater.

Friends are coming over for tea,
I shall tell them, 'Now I'm three.'

Candles on the cake, biscuits on the plate,
Time for a party, I can't wait.

It's been a long day, being three,
But at least these presents . . .
       . . . belong to *me!*

Rachel Cross

Wild Friends

When I come down in the morning
I watch the bluetits ride,
On my hanging birdfeeder,
As they peck the nuts inside.

They seem quite oblivious
Of being under observation,
And feed until they are startled,
Flying away in consternation.

Then there is a blackbird,
Who chides me when I go down,
To fill his container with water,
Before I go shopping in the town.

There's also a bright-eyed robin,
Who keeps me company,
Ready to snatch any worms or beetles,
I can offer for his family.

In the afternoon a lady,
With her old dog passes by,
And he always laps gratefully,
At the dog bowl on his way.

Any scraps I may have,
I throw onto the grass,
For the jackdaws in the chimneypots,
To gather in a swift pass.

Suzanna Wilson

Richard Griffin

Today I heard
The news
That we had lost a friend
This devastating blow
Is hard for us
To even comprehend.

We wish it
Never came to this
For us to say goodbye
To someone
That we cherished
It's hard to even try.

You filled the day
With laughter
You were a kind and gentle soul
It's hard for us
To say goodbye
It's hard to let you go.

In honour
Of your memory
A poem to you, from us,
You mean the world
To us all
And we love you very much.

Barbara C Perkins

Book Of Dreams

So I couldn't dream in colour, no noise to start me awake,
I could see the waves though as they broke upon the shore,
The futility of a love affair, her heart, when to forsake,
My innermost thoughts revealed, my dreams tell so much more.

Not dreams in the day, only at the dead of night,
Foretells of meeting someone you were not expected to see again,
Whether a blessing or tragic, I prayed for the day to light,
Movement so rapid in my eyes, yet ne'er to see the rain.

A disaster if not to overwhelm, eventual triumph, cold to touch,
A storm-ravaged lake, from troubled slumber I awoke,
The sea breezes, sand trickles through my fingers, no pain as such,
I am to be used to advance another's interests, again no joke.

Through waist-high meadow grasses I tentatively walk,
Caressing the flowers, alone, no bees, no birds, no trace,
A season of plenty, provides for the future, no noises nor talk,
I wonder, would that be Heaven, no stranger a place.

Warm sun upon my face, springtime maybe, wildlife and the trees,
Polar opposites, darkness, tunnel of emptiness and ill will,
A favourable omen for lovers and new business, no stormy seas,
With a smile on my lips I awoke as winter rains lashed my sill.

I spoke to my grandfather once, my father's father, it seemed so real,
In pain, long since departed, I asked him what he was doing here,
He smiled, truly at peace, strength and courage I could feel,
It was so real, that dream, as I wiped away the tear.

Michael Hartshorne

My Special Friend

Memories of friendship brings one person to mind
A lovely, gentle being, so patient and so kind
Always there to listen whether it was day or night
Trying to give solutions to that current plight

She was so understanding, she always helped me through
Her ideas were priceless when I didn't have a clue
That was so many years ago, she is now far away
But her wisdom is still with me to help through a bad day

I took her for granted, never thinking she would leave
But the day came too soon when for her I had to grieve
I had a friend and mother all wrapped into one
Not realising how lucky I was until the day she'd gone

Not everyone is fortunate to have a special friend
She always made me smile bringing my cares to an end
Treasure the gift that is free, remember there's no cost
For tomorrow it could vanish, leaving you empty and lost

Barbara Lambie

The Childhood Friend

I miss the simplicity of our conversations,
Our fits of hysterical laughter on the tiniest occasions.
I miss you, and your smile and your glow.
I miss not having you there whenever I'm feeling down or low,
To automatically pick me up again without even trying to.
I miss the confidence boost you give me when you're around,
The crazy whirlwind view of life you have.
The fun we have.

Caroline Foster

Best Friend Grandma

Thanks grandma
For being there
Through thick and thin

When I am down
You are always giving
Me strength to succeed

Always available on
The phone 24/7
Day or night

I can speak
To you about
Anything I wish

You are my
Best friend grandma
In the whole world.

Bav

Empty

I walk along an empty beach,
My thoughts of you but you're out of reach.
I wish you were here to hold my hand
But there's only miles of empty sand.

The waves are crashing on the shore,
Our love, it is no more.
I walk into an empty cave,
Our love, I could not save.

As I turn and walk away,
I could have sworn I heard someone say
    'Don't worry.'

Sandra Softley

For The Duration . . .

Mother's Arms

When the night draws over her darkness
And the moon and stars, weeping silver tears,
Drip-shatter upon Man's oblivion
The Earth dares stretch, tormented
Tending septic wounds

And rain falls clear and sweet, until a gentle breeze
Breathes calm . . . through trees beckoning, 'Come'
A skirting brook dances unscaled harmonies through this veil
upon veil
While an owl, stark staring, asks nature's question . . . 'Who?'

So, to and fro' in cyclical, turns each night until
With crescendo Clash, then soft and slow
Sunlight . . . bakes warm . . . break day

Why then, oh Man, to raise your head
No thought to stop and pray?

Taariq Crossley

My Darling Boy Kai

My darling boy, I love you so
When you were born
I counted all your fingers and toes.

I kissed your downy head and touched your button nose
The love was instant and painful too;
With an unbreakable bond between us two
For I had created the most perfect artwork in you.

Your smile is like the sun
And your tears like the rain
When you feel hurt I feel pain
It is a privilege to watch you grow, that is true
For I have created the most perfect artwork in you.

Lorraine Jones

Writer's Block

Fresh page, new start
Story told from the heart
Words fail, don't fit
Throw away what's writ.

Fresh page, start again
White space, idle pen
Verbs, nouns don't knit
Throw away what's writ.

Fresh page, another try
Plot, theme, wave goodbye
Bright idea not lit
Throw away what's writ

Bestseller, sure-fire hit?
Can't read what's not writ.

Nettie Thomson

My Love For Mary

My love for Mary
Not easily stated
But complicated
Like her
Like her

My love for Mary
Never departed
Just broken-hearted
Like her
Like her

My love for Mary
Too desperately given
Lies unforgiven
Like me
Like me.

Jeff Mearns

For The Duration . . .

Don't Look Back!

Don't look back when you say goodbye
I've set you free to let you fly
You've got your aims and goals to score
Rugby, cricket and lots more.

Please do your best to pass all tests
And don't forget to wear your vest!
This way of life will be so new
But I'll always find time to think of you.

You've grown a lot over the years that have passed
Buildng blocks, Lego no more at last!
Time to experiment with our new-found life
At times there will be trouble, no doubt strife.

Try to be strong and always do your best
Be kind to others, and you will be blessed
Your future is bright and whatever lies ahead
Your home is here and enough has been said.

Mandi Evans

Yesterday

My PC coughed up a name out of the blue -
Conjuring you, conjuring *us* up.

Together we did nothing spectacular:
Laughed a lot; ate strange dishes I saw born;
Learnt to disinter breakfast from warm ash,
Went with you to a special plot among photographs
And scrawls   one day . . .

What days!
A child and mother as one.

What nights
Conjoined at the hip.

(certain foods placed in dying ash cook by morning)

Oliver Cox

Lost Love

The thunder of the ocean filled my heart with rapturous applause.
As the crashing of the waves with white feathers roared.
Both day and night with a relentless purging at the bay of your heart.
With a strength of passion no man could enfold.
Complete not corrupt,
And so pure in essence and strength of flight.

As the earth needs the trees to take root, a passion creeps over
                                                  The earth.
Contagious, and clamped within the jaws of the reptile,
Gripped so tight,
No release could ever evolve.

As the body needs a soul to embark into a journey to paradise,
Like time in flight.
As a jigsaw needs a puzzle
And a puzzle needs a hole
(No man can disprove).
This undiluted passion, intoxicating mirth.
How it lives to quench the unquenchable thirst,
To make this body whole.

And so, to view with baited breath the completion of this Earth-born man.
The embodiment of manhood?
Wholistic enterty?
How a complexity of desire provokes the segments within the soul.
Just as the part of you that loves me
Sits softly on the tree, like a sparrow ready for flight
Looking straight into ecstasy.
But as the moonlight flickers watching jade across the woodland,
With clouds that hide its black flight
I turn around to see sunlight

With a crackling of undergrowth so hard beneath my feet.
And I fall from flight.
Shot with a precision so precise
No salvage can repair.
As my blood-splattered plumage hits the ground
The beauty of my flight in glory,
Is lost for eternity.
Continuum in essence.

Christine Flowers

Shattered Dreams

They lit the touch clothe of my heart,
Blowing all of my dreams apart,
To hit the ground like shattered glass,
That someone with a hammer smashed,
I look on as they lie all around,
In them no hope at all can be found,
I try to mend the tattered parts,
To once again fix my broken heart,
It seems that I am missing a vital part,
Upon my knees I search, in an effort to find,
This thing that they all call peace of mind,
Somehow it is gone along with my trust,
To seek for it I feel that I really must,
Only to discover that it cannot be replaced,
For within my mouth there lives a bitter taste,
I have lost my dreams, now that's a waste.

Pauline Uprichard

Love

That elusive experience we've named as love,
Which can be fierce as a lion or gentle as a dove.
We long for it, dream of it, chase after it -
Our souls are uplifted, our faces are lit!

So why do we crave this feeling called love?
The fabric of dreams with it can be wove.
Our cup of joy overflows when it's in our sights,
We can drop to the depths, or soar to the heights!

No reason or rhyme to the pattern of love -
It sneaks up behind us and gives us a shove!
When we're looking for love it cannot be found,
But try giving up on it, and it arrives without sound!

What comprises the make-up of this thing called love?
Passionate, incandescent light sent from above!
A feeling that rages and becomes heart's desire -
It can make us feel blue, or fill us with fire!

Love, love, love - it enriches our souls -
Enhances our certainty of life, and our roles.
Person to person - enjoining us, and forging a link,
For such, we'll take our chances, to swim or to sink!

However barren yet busy our lives may become,
However hard we school our hearts to be numb.
The unexpected moment love sneaks up and finds a way in,
We open our hearts to the coveted prize we always could win!

Lorena Valerie Owens

Love

A small and simple word it seems
Which conjures up a world of dreams
And yet to know and touch and feel
We know full well it's all for real.

For love is so immeasurable
And to the brim is always full
Sometimes on impulse it may move
And act upon its strength to prove.

For love is something here within
It has no room for doubt or sin
A kindly deed or thought or smile
Makes everything seem more worthwhile.

Love hath no barriers, nor is found
To force upon - or to be bound
It's always there to enrich and bless
In a world where there is much distress.

Love gives all - expects nothing in return
Never counts the cost - and has money to burn
Patience and understanding all seem to form
Right from the very day we were born.

So if you have love in your heart, be glad
And thankful as not to be sad;
For God is Love - its origin
Tell others - and seek hearts to win.

Gillian Morgan

Love At Mrs Bridges

At first glance
As you walked in,
Shaded by the café door.

Slight and slim
As willow in
The raglan coat you wore.

Love struck deep,
Pierced right through me,
Left me drowning in despair.

Pale silk-skinned
Pre-Raphaelite,
With cascading Titian hair;

There was beauty
Shining from you,
Siddons eyes could not compare.

You I love
And promise truly,
Only you for evermore.

Robert King

Recollection

A year has gone; the Earth has moved
And stars and planets in their courses.
The birds' dawn chorus, note on note
Revives the aura that was you.
The dove-grey cloud above is rent
By one long silvered gash of pearl
Till pursued by a high flying breeze
The ragged edges blend and heal.
Below is stillness
And beauty of memories . . .

Eric Gladwin

Bearer Of Butterflies

You're the life and soul of my party
You're the joker in every pack
You're an opinionated free spirit
And I've always got your back
For you I have to kill the craving
For you I have to bury the feeling
You say friends is all we can be
I wish you could see potential in me.

You're the bearer of butterflies in my stomach
A glimmer of light in a day that feels dark
You're a sensitive soul and the world doesn't know.
You're the only one who doesn't see our spark
For you I have to disguise the pining
For you I have to numb the yearning
You say friends is all we can be
I wish you could find a love in me.

P Dixon

Love

Put your arms around me darling,
Hold me close
And never let me go
Keep me in your mind forever
And forever, and never forget me.

I've loved you so much,
I cannot bear to touch you
I've known you so long.
I seemed to have lost track of the time.
It's only dawned on me today
For tomorrow's another day.

Florence Greener

Love

Love, love, is the greatest gift we can share.
Without love, it would be just me, and not you.
For with love, I share with you.
My love is no longer with me,
But in the arms of love Himself, God above.
True love never dies,
But lasts for eternity.
As it has been said,
Better to have loved and lost,
Than to never have loved at all.
Love, love, is the greatest gift of all.
Through God's love, we came into being,
And He gave us love so we could share
And care for one another.
Jesus' love has set us free
Because He went to Calvary
And died upon the tree
Because only His blood could set us free.
True love never thinks of self,
But puts others, before self,
Love, love is the answer to all our cares,
For true love shares,
Love creates, never destroys
Love always builds up,
Never tears down.
For true love always shares and cares,
God's love joined man and woman
Together to be one flesh
This is a great mystery
Only God knows, this mystery
For God is love.

Stanley Moore

For The Duration . . .

I Will Remember

I look up to the sky
And see the stars above
That is where I know you are
My love

I know as I look up
That you look down at me
So until we meet again
I will keep you in my heart
And all our treasured memories
I will retain

The things we did and said
Always saying goodnight before bed
Random thoughts in my head
As down memory lane I'm led

Without you life can never be the same
But into my life I'm glad you came
And never the like to meet again

I will see you in my dreams
And feel you when awake
Something from me nothing can ever take

For all the loved ones
We will never forget
And are forever grateful
That by fate we met.

Anne Brodie

Making A Break For It - No-Man's-Land

I've been stuck down here with you
In the trenches, in a marriage as grey as mud,
Stuck down here as the rats of revenge
Scurry back and forth in the crud.
Stuck down here where it's safe and quiet,
Quiet as Hell as we sulk and squirm,
Gnawing at the bones of ancient battles,
And raking over the coals of despair,
Where might-have-beens and should-haves
Hover and glow in the sulphurous air;
Stuck down here while the roaches of grudge
Scrabble and scratch in dark corners;
The moths of tit for tat thump away at dim lamps,
And patches of grim annoyance blotch the walls,
Stuck down here waiting for the bitter end,
An end that can't come too soon.
So maybe tomorrow I will cut and run,
Scramble up the banks into open fields
Where the guns belch fire and people die,
Where you take your chances as cannon fodder
Up in the no-man's-land of modern life!

Liz Davies

It's Love

It spreads just like being bitten by a bug
Not dissimilar to an infectious disease
It takes its own medication and time to recover
The first experience can never be repeated.

Margot Reich

No More Of This

No more of this: I'll not be tuning forever
To your comings and goings, surging my tide
Of consciousness, stirring to restless fever

The shore-break pulse. I will be cool and please
Explicitly myself in placid pools
Of unruffled disdain. I'll not release

And wanton my strict soul in base surrender
To a common need. Intact, I'll not adapt
My life to your agenda, I'll not squander

All on one - dreaming, planning, grieving
Briefly all for one. Not even briefly
Immersed till use would be bereaving

Both of passion, would blunt desire by taking,
Threadbare lust to a habit. I will suppress
The longing in me, the void, the desolate aching.

Still your coming and going surge my tide
Of consciousness, quickening to a fever
The shore-break pulse. As will had broken, died.

Kate Lyons

Ty

You're the one I rely on
You're the man I love
There's nothing I want more
Than to be the one you love and trust
You hold me so tightly I can hardly breathe
You make me feel so protected I never want to leave
You make me feel confident, happy and free
You make me so happy it's hard to believe
I love you my darling so very much
I never want a second to pass without your loving touch.

Janice Bailey

The Girl Of My Dreams

At last our hardship has ended,
And our dreary long task is through,
Now this broken heart shall be mended,
In Liverpool, sweet Ellen with you.

I'll forget those extremes, with the girl of my dreams,
When the Liver Birds light up, and then,
We'll stroll and we'll dream, 'neath the silver moonbeam
When the moon lights the Mersey again.

For I know in my heart, that we'll never part,
When you change your sweet name to mine.
Our love like the river, shall flow on forever,
Sweet Ellen, my angel divine.

I'll forget those extremes, with the girl of my dreams,
When the Liver Birds light up, and then,
We'll stroll and we'll dream, 'neath the silver moonbeam,
When the moon lights the Mersey again,
'Liverpool', when the moon lights the Mersey again.

James Baxter

Soulmate

I pay tribute to the one that has become my soulmate
We laugh of how I made her wait.

Always there in time of support and need
One of energy, laughter and caring deed.

Wife, mother, neighbour and friend
A Christian faith leading her to give and lend.

Her short part in history she plays
Making us and me part of richer days.

So much to say and no word to express
Perhaps simply thank you and may God bless.

Clive Cornwall

A Cautious Approach

I have always worn my heart on my sleeve.
But are my senses being deceived?
Each night of late the Earth and sky
Seem to echo the fire of love. But I am wary
Because if I put my trust in a woman, would it be sheer folly?
Yet she tells me she loves me, I do like her
But I'm not made for heartache
Then when the image of her beautiful face comes to me
All my self-doubts are erased
And sweet thoughts calm my unsteady heart
Yet how disconcerting that her flashing eyes can quickly disarm me
Oh vulnerable heart, do you trust her? If so why do you dither,
She won't wait forever
Yes! I must reach for her now and summon the courage to tell her
I love her,
Then in hope I will place her hand into mine.
And wish with all my heart that love alone would end in contentment.

Tony Beeby

Crush

You're making my heart beat faster
And taking my breath away
Trying hard not to think about you
Every second of every day

Hiding my feelings from you
Too scared for you to find out
Just how much I like you
In case you get freaked out

My sun is always shining
Even if I'm feeling blue
All of this just happens
Whenever I see or think of you.

Chloe Catlin

Untitled

You know Dear Lord some time ago I gave my heart to You,
You cared for it and filled it up with love so strong and true
It made me change my way of life and see it through Your eyes,
Compassion, love for all I met I tried to emphasise.

Grant me the strength to carry on and show what I can do,
To prove to others day by day my heart belongs to You
Give them the sight to see in me just how You made me whole,
A servant given all I need to reach that Heavenly goal.

I must admit I feel some guilt in what I now confess,
It isn't that my love for You is feeling any less,
But someone else has stolen my heart away from me
And therefore Lord I need a new or bigger heart You see.

I know You know of Rosemary as you sent her to my side
In answer to my prayer when I asked you be my guide,
I am sure you will consider how to deal with my request
And grant me love enough to share I'm sure you'll do your best.

So forgive me Lord for I am sure you really know
That I'm not deserting You at all, that's not my wish, and so
I hope You understand me and why I pray to You
To make my heart grow bigger so I can share my love with two.

David North

For The Duration . . .

O Love Of My Heart

You are a beauty before my eyes,
A rare jewel in a golden crown
And it's with love that I turn to you
To touch, caress and to kiss.

Swathed in majesty you look divine,
For my heart seeks your beauty,
And yet a place is waiting for you
A special place of peace and rest within.

You who turn the heads of kings and queens,
Even children so gay smile at you
You wear your heart upon your sleeve
And your love is known before men!

In my mind you are a crowned princess,
Princess of the seven veils
With ruby lips and eyes that sparkle
In a moment we both shall kiss.

Lady of my heart's desire,
For in you I have fallen in love
You have captivated my heart and soul
And with mercy I give the greatest of pleasures.

Simon Foderingham

I Love You Forever And A Day

I love you, I love you, and I know you love me
I love you, I love you like a bird in a tree
I know that you love me, I won't fly away
I'll love you, I'll love you forever and a day.

I love you like a rabbit in a field of corn
I know that I loved you ever since I was born
If I know that you love me I won't burrow away
I'll love you, I'll love you forever and a day.

I love you like a mole who is under the ground
Who drills through his tunnel without making a sound
He works in his tunnels so dismal and dark
If he knows that you love him he could sing like a lark

I love you like a dog who is faithful and true
You can tell by his eyes that he only loves you
If you tell him you love him then come what may
He'll love you forever, forever and a day

I love you, I love you, and I know you love me
I love you, I love you like the bird in the tree
Like the rabbit in the cornfield I know you love me
I love you like the mole who sings in the dark
I love you like the dog who can only just bark

I love you, I love you and I know you love me
I love you, I love you forever I'll stay
I'll love you forever, forever and a day.

Lionel Brown

The Coming Of Summer

Summer smiles her sweet romance,
On close liaison, quite by chance,
Breath of love that draws us in,
Hearts are open, let's begin.
Seek your hand to enfold mine,
Fingers eager to entwine,
Need and Want implied as such,
All revealed in that first touch.
Summer's silence hears our sighs
And whispered nothings; close my eyes
To feel you touching me and mine,
Feather-like along my spine.
Stroking, smoothing, yielding lair,
Heady fragrance fills the air,
Lips exploring come to rest
On lover's flushed and rising breast.
Veil of warmth that's gossamer thin,
Washes over our salty skin,
Ebb and flow of our endeavour,
Waves of passion, ride together.
Love be still! And then subside,
Lying languid, side by side,
As Summer came, and then did fade,
Her smile remained and love was made.

Val Haslam

Just Like Lovers Do

Your love was always there for me
In everything I'd do
We travelled together on this road
Just like lovers do.

And when you felt
You had followed me
Just as far as you could go

I can tell you now
It nearly broke my heart
Just to watch you go

And no matter where you travel
We will never be apart
As I will always love you
With all of my heart

Your love was always
There for me
In everything I'd do
We travelled together
On this road
Just like lovers do.

K Lake

A Mother's Love
(For James)

I know you so well. You are my child
I know your thoughts, your dreams, your hopes, your fears.
I cry when you cry, I hurt when you hurt,
Because you are my child.

I remember so well when you were small.
I would sit you on my knee and tell you
Everything will be alright
I could kiss your pains away then.

My love for you is always there, just as it always was.
It will never go out of sight.
Because you are my child.

You will never be alone. How can you be?
You are locked into a corner of my heart.
There is never a day, an hour, minute or second
That you leave my thoughts,
Because you are my child.

I am here for you when life's turmoils and despairs
Sometimes overtake you.
Just call me . . . I love you dearly,
Because you are my child.

Christine Jean Venour

Soldier's Loving Embrace

As I wait to go into battle I remember your angelic face,
And I hope at the end of this time and place,
I will live to hold you in my arms' embrace,
Instead of this weapon of wars destructive embrace.
And I pray the good Lord will set me free from this deadliest place
And this is my pledge that I give to you
If I live to get out of this place to love you for evermore
In this soldier's loving embrace.

Reply
O my soldier of love, I hope you come through that deadly place
Without a scratch on any place.
And I can hold you once more in a soft embrace.
For you and me in this most precious state.
As I dread you going back to that war-like place.
And I pray the loving God keeps you for me in His most precious safe place
of love to share, till we meet again
In this soldier's loving embrace.

J B Watkinson

An Ode To My Love

Sapping, sapping slightly at the wind
My love so sweetly gives her bid
Call me thus, and keep me true
I whisper back, her eyes so blue

My heart pounding, like the fall of rain
She gives me the sweetest pain
Oh my love, let me into your sweet showers
Embrace me with your God-given powers

I drink my fill, washing down my veins
She buffets madly, letting go her reins
On my love swims inside my heart so true
Who commands it, me or you?

Natalie Williams

For The Duration . . .

Better To Have Loved You At All

That I have seen rather than missed,
That I have heard rather than ignored,
That I have tasted rather than avoided,
That I have smelt rather than shunned.

That I have ran rather than walked,
That I have sighed rather than breathed,
That I have wept rather than watched,
That I have feared rather than fled.

That I have touched rather than dismissed,
That I have longed rather than rejected,
That I have despaired rather than abandoned,
That I have dreamt rather than forgotten.

Better to have known you at all,
Better to have loved you at all.

Danielle Ward

To . . .

(From one who is sometimes bowled over)

I take it as a compliment
To my good luck in having you
When people say how good you look,
Because, we being two,
I think perhaps I can't be bad,
A lad who's complement to you.

Your character is sterling as your looks
Though 'sterling' refers to silver in my books
And you are good as gold,
Not 'goody-goody' but very kind,
And good to have and hold
Till death is left behind
- But I grow over-bold!

Rich rich Bard

Eternal

I wait for the day when I shall find the one meant for me,
My eternal love,
My eternal dream,
And whilst I know you are still far off,
I cannot help but to dream of you,
To ponder what you shall be like,
What you will hold for me,
I am waiting for you my love,
Because until the day I find you,
I fear I shall not be able to love another,
You are the special someone it takes to unlock my heart,
For me to once again be able to trust another,
Truly trust another,
With my life, my love, my soul.
I yearn to wake up one day and find you were not a dream,
But that you are a reality.
My reality.
To feel the embrace I've longed for,
To hear the voice I've searched for.
I do not see your face, or hear your voice,
Whence I am dreaming of you,
I only know that the day you are here,
I will know.

Jennifer Mobley

Dreams Of Yesterday

Footsteps, echoing from room to room
Remind me, you were gone too soon
And yet not gone,
For memories linger on
Of dreams of yesterday.

Your voice, silent, yet I hear
A whisper, telling me you're near
Guiding, watchful, loving still
And always sharing
Dreams of yesterday.

Your smiling face I cannot see
And yet I know you're near to me,
Your gentle hands caress me still
And you I see in
Dreams of yesterday.

When one has known a love like ours
It blossoms like the sweetest flowers,
Yet dies not, for all time it will be
Forever there
In dreams of yesterday.

But are they dreams or just God's way
To ease the loneliness each day?
My darling whatsoere they be
They bring thoughts to me
Of love of yesterday.

Lillian Derry

Look Away

Hide your eyes from me,
Your words are cold,
You look away,
False words betrayed by destiny
Don't you say 'You look nice today'
Hide your eyes from me
For the tale they tell
Of suffering and Hell.
Struggling with agonising pain
Forbidden love has stuck again!
We go our separate ways.
But etched on the tree of my soul!
The love that won't die
Timeless, eternal, God's intervention
Let no man question!
I kiss to forget you!
In passionless arms!
I dance till the sunrise!
I smoke till the dawn!
Praying to God, love be gone!

Jessie Shields

Heartbroken

I have my legs, though I cannot walk
I have a heart but it doesn't beat anymore
I have my speech
Though I cannot talk
The words I love you don't come out anymore

I have my eyes, though I cannot see
The way you used to smile at me
I have the sense of touch, though I cannot feel
Your arms wrapped tightly around me

I have my ears, though I cannot hear
Your voice calling out to me
I have my lips to put lipstick upon
Though kisses from you, they are long gone

My nerves are shaky and my confidence is gone
I feel lonely and depressed
Since you've been gone.

When I think back
To when we first met
I don't have a single regret.

Annette Foreman

All My Love

I've loved a lot, lived many years,
Filled with laughter, joy and tears,
Mum and Dad and brothers - two -
How I thought the world of you,
Surrounded by uncles, aunties, cousins,
Lots of friends - there must be dozens,
Friends from school, at work and play
All I've gathered along life's way.

My next love was the best of all and I became his wife,
It was the beginning of a very different life.
We loved each other dearly - I learned to love his folks
Life was full of laughter - he played so many jokes.
Then came along the children - two daughters and a son.
More love to give and cherish, and new lives had begun.
I thought it would last forever - but no - 'twas not to be
My love was taken ill and sadly went from me.
What would I do without him? How often did I cry
But I had to keep on going - that's life - with many a sigh.

My family was so helpful - they too had loved and lost
A father good, steadfast and true - they also count the cost.
My daughters then were married - began another life,
Our son was much too busy to find himself a wife.
The love just kept on growing - I'm Grandma now you see,
To four of the loveliest grandchildren you always hope will be.
I love them very dearly - I've watched them grow and thrive,
It would have been so perfect with my husband by my side.

They're older now, and so am I - more grief has come my way,
For then I lost my only son - another very sad day.
He was so very poorly - I shed so many tears
I know it was much worse for him, his illness lasted years.
I hope that he is with his dad, wherever that may be,
To have a chat and reminisce, and sometimes think of me.

My daughters do a lot for me, the love is still so strong,
They take me out and come to stay, it's gone on for so long.
Their children also keep in touch, their busy lives they share,
They send their love - it means so much - just to know they care.
And so the love keeps growing, I hope it always will,
Then this old heart will be content when, at last, it's still.

Edna Ratcliffe

Loving The Real Time

Summer began, and it was beautiful,
We could have walked forever, really, we should have,
But I had the wrong shoes on and had to turn back.

It felt right to hold your hand, and you didn't seem to mind,
When we passed that bridal shop, we danced,
You to your beat and me to mine.

Two girls came along and wanted to be friends, we chatted and smiled.
You were warm and funny
But I knew we were out of touch.

The night closed in too quickly, gathering past emotion,
It wasn't just us, but them,
Love, a sweet expectation.
But we'd lost the connection by then.

When I looked today, you were still there,
Though not physically, your sensual voice fading
Like those unwanted apples at the foot of your tree.

Tracey Cornwell

Linda

Too late for dreams, the alarm is going off,
I sit up and get dressed, oh God life is tough
Go down the stairs, let the dogs go outside!
Put on the kettle, it's breakfast time.

Fill a bowl of cereal, just eat and then
Dogs are at the door so I let them back in
Now the kettle has boiled so I make me a brew
Get down two cups, must not forget about you!

I have a sip of mine first then it's back upstairs
I call out your name, you're still lying there!
You then start to move and sit up real slow
I say, 'Here is your cuppa, don't let it go cold.'

You say, 'Just a minute you're forgetting something!'
You pucker your lips up and give me a grin
I give you a kiss and a cuddle as well
Life is not so bad really, in fact it is quite swell!

L J Roche

Reminiscences Torment My Past Endeavours

Confused echoes of the distant past plagues my mind
Great expectations, so long ago now out of sight
Imagined fulfilments, so clear then only if fate were kind
Now just memories barely alive
Were fancied certs, though finances tight
The loves, the doubts, remain my mystical imaginary dreams
Out of reach, like a rainbow's end!
The good life, always elusive, like a famous pot of gold
Constant thoughts, that disturb never stand a chance to mend
Only future fate, that's lucky will forever persist
If genuinely taught
Though thoughts unexpressed, not told will cancel clemency sought.

Brian Wharmby

Mum

Mum, I never told you
That I loved you so.
I thought no words were needed,
I thought that you would know.

And now it's too late,
To say the words to you.
But just in case you're listening,
I'll say them, 'I love you.'

I'm glad that I knew you,
For twelve years of my life.
You will always be remembered,
As our mother and Dad's wife.

So Mum, I'll see you later,
In the place up in the sky.
I know you will be waiting,
So just for now, 'Goodbye.'

Gillian Fitzsimmons

Broken Hearts
(For Roberto and Gino born sleeping 13/8/06)

Two little babies lying side by side
Leaving hearts broken, leaving us behind
Only God knows best, why you had to go
But leaving us behind leaves us full of woe.

Two little babies playing in Heaven's clouds
Happy and smiling, without a care in the world
They don't know we are crying down here below
Broken shells of what we were but we know you had to go.

My two little babies, if only you both knew
How hard it is without you and hard for a brother too
For we will never forget you, our world just fell apart
And I only hope and pray that you can mend our broken hearts.

Anne Green

One Romantic Night

Close in each other's arms
We swayed to the waltz
Your laughter and voice
A melodious symphony of sound
I clung to your body replete in our embrace
Wishing mine would melt into yours
I love your hair,
Your earlobe, and face
I am tempted to trace, but I settle
For the graceful curve of your neck
As I place on it a loving kiss
I breathe in your scent
Not of the aftershave but of you
You gaze into my eyes and I'm in Heaven
I am not afraid to express my love
Because we have been made one
The soothing music and the candlelit room
Destabilise my senses
I can feel your body next to mine
Virile and alive as we share a kiss
As we continue to dance into the night.

Debra Valley

In Love Again

A look, a smile
A voice, a stare
Her walk, her eyes
Her flowing hair

You can't think
You can't speak
You can't breathe
You can't eat . . . you're in love

You plan your next meeting
Your off the cuff greeting
The smiles that you share
Your heart is aware . . . you're in love

You share the wind, the rain and the snow
Not feeling cold, both hearts aglow
Beating as one
As if under the sun . . . you're in love

Time stands still till you see her again
The waiting
The longing
The pain . . . you're in love.

Ryszard Lipinski

The Lychgate

I have no imagery for time's passing
Beyond the memory of a rendezvous -
With those moments I have come to cherish -
Except in retrospect where a curious
Poignancy retrieves a carved memento
Of dedication; the traces of which
Remain as my nostalgia that lingers
With its sentiment. An edifice of
Solemnity now looms on limbs that bare
That heart - a deeper grain is etched along
The timber - that arched accompaniment
Brought together with a canopy that
Gives this gothic masterpiece distinction.
By some irony it assumes the last of
That provision for solace albeit
Fleeting as that kiss before departing.
It witnesses a brief affair - a heart,
A life - that oak from several centuries.

William Birtwistle

For The Duration . . .

Love's Power

Love is the most powerful force in the universe.
It's never strained or perverse.
It breaks even the most powerful curse
And before it all problems disperse.

The stars above us dance for joy.
The moon is like a child's toy.
When we meet as girl and boy
There will be no need for us to be coy.

Our love will forever last.
Our foolish ways aside we'll cast.
Bury our sorrows of the past
And nail our colours to the mast.

Love will fulfil us in good time.
So long as we commit no crime.
Our life together will be sublime
But now it's time to end this rhyme.

Philip Tucker

Why?

Something to think about now and forever,
I will never understand why.

We could have had it all together,
Why did you throw it away?

We made the sun shine even when it was raining,
Why did you throw it away?

We had what it takes to be happy forever,
Why did you throw it away?

Never forget I love you more than the sun can shine,
More than the rain can fall,

More than you will ever know,
If I told you ever day it would never be enough,

That's how much I love you now and always will,

Why did you throw *me* away?

Why?

I will never understand.

Christine Vincent

No Honeymoon

A broken heart
From a broken 'dream'.
A love affair
That was, just
Me and you.
Forever in time!
On cloud nine.
Then the winds of change
Whisked us apart.
We never heed'd
Their moanful sigh.
If we could have tomorrow
As we had 'yesterday'
Could our feet
Stay firmly on the ground?
Or would the memories
The music of yesteryear
Be a dream too far?
As the winds of change
Dashed our hopes
For a rainbow's end
To that wonderful romance.

Margaret Parnell

Victoria

Your loving eyes look into mine
Dear love feels so fine
I am pleased you are mine oh mine
I know I met you just in time
Time really so very quick
But love lasts all through time
Love so sweet, love so fine
It's like milk and honey
All the time
You mean so very much to me
That is how it should be
A love that's for evermore
Inside my head burns a fire
You're the one that I desire
It will burn bright tonight
As I hold you tight.

Gordon Forbes

True Wisdom

Heart of the unknown flows deeply
Within the realm of wisdom,
Seeing a thesis in the clouds,
Reading poetry in the trees,
Imagery of the mind told.
Feelings that betray you,
Sincere wishes unspoken,
Secures all inner love,
Hearing echoes in your soul.
Your mind engages; true wisdom.

Cecil Hickman

Benignly Affected

Your sweet voice.
Tender spring;
Musing past the avalanche
Of my mind.

Subtle shades of hue,
Caressing raw elements,
Cool to touch;

Day breaks.
A polyphony of sound -
The twitter of morning song.

The hope I find as passively
I await your beckoning clutch.

Arriving I dissipate
The entanglement of my mind;
Discovering in-turn
An evolved notion of the good.

Hooked, I succumb to such a
Multiplicity of forces.
Washing away, discarding
The memory of time.

At once, now that my senses
Are numbed;
We are together, united
As one.
Grateful for this good!

Stephen Shutak

Living

I went with you, walking
Our voices merged, stalking
The moment in which our beings, living
Intermingled and dwelt, fighting
As two co-existence demands, compromising
And as war will dictate, forgiving
So that as we sit, thinking
Energy and will diminished, resting
I turn and I see you, loving
And I remember the sounds, rustling
Of your legs through the sheets, f**king
And your gasps on the air, gulping
And how we were so much more, creating
And I turn to ye gods, thanking
For love, 'tis not in the death but the living.

Jonathan Potter

Crush

There is a thunderous roar in my head
Like someone is pounding to get out,
The blood rushes to my brain,
Tearing away my mask, so there will be no shred of doubt
The true me is forced to the surface,
My cheeks flame a bright red,
My knees feel weak, and I almost stumble,
Suddenly thoughts cascade through my head.
When will this all be over?
When will my mind no longer be infringed?
Let me get over this childish crush,
Otherwise I will come completely unhinged.

Kimberly Harries

Forever

Alas! if you would have seen this before you left me
Is there any array needed to know this?
I found myself always in the dream that you are mine,
I never knew it was just a shine, which
I saw ever in your eyes! But it wasn't mine!

Recalling the days which I passed with you,
Living in the hope I might come back to you!
I am scared for the past,
The fate which snatched you
May not take you much more last!

My mind says you are a fool,
My heart reminds me to be cool!
I know you are away from me,
Even your dreams may discard me,
Gone forever, never to return,
If I have hope what is Saturn?

If you wish to remember me in the future
Just look back once, I may be there!
Waiting for you, now and forever!
'Cause you know you are mine forever!

Awadhut M Shiwankar

Ensconced Therein

Ensconced therein her velvet skin,
The kindest heart that knew not sin;
And blessed am I, for I did win,
The pure sweet love ensconced therein.

Keith Miller

Love

Beneath the starlit sky and moon above,
A secluded place, I chose to pledge my troth.
No one to hear my tender words of love.
A love I hope will bring such joy to both.

'Will you be mine?' I whisper in her ear
As moving close we let our hands entwine.
I feel a glowing warmth as she draws near
And holds her trembling body close to mine.

I gaze into her eyes as they meet mine
And try to read the very thoughts within.
Clear as crystal do they shine.
A knowing smile evolves into a grin.

She answers yes and with delight
We saunter onward through the night.

Maureen Beaumont

True Love

Don't give up on things that make you smile
make all your life worth living worthwhile

You may be standing on different floors
but you'll always love them behind closed doors

Love is something that should last forever
you'll always love and grow up together

Sometimes it might not work and if it doesn't
You will look them in the eye
And say, 'It can't be the end, I won't say goodbye.'

Stacey Wreford (14)

My Valentine

I wished he had sent me a card, such a long time ago
Those days now thinking, even now when I just let him go
Such a foolish heart through our very young days
A guardsman to be proud of, in so many, many ways

Just letting him out of my fingers, was told time and time again
Now knowing he was my valentine, was rather quite a shame
Now to living with memories, whilst sitting by the firelight side
Thinking of those times we shared, and thoughts that cannot hide

Those times we shared, through those golden hours
As we danced, around the glorious flowers
Whilst the band was playing, in the park
While, listening and watching a to perky lark

Gliding to the sky, settling five minutes on the ground
Disappearing again, listening to his flute-like sound
Watching his movements, as the band played on
While sitting by the riverside, watching the swans glide along

Till the afternoon went by, the sun disappeared
When the moon shone bright, as evening appeared
We shared a loving kiss, under the starry night
Arms around each other, as we bid a goodnight

Those thoughts are still with me, from time to time
When receiving a special card, for this valentine
This day to remember as time goes by
Let a special love shine, like those stars in the sky

A valentine card is special, even from a young loved one
Even through time, till the day is done
Even when golden days creep on, and time may fly by
Just like the sweetness of nature, like the birds that fly.

Jean McGovern

On The Battlefields Of Love

There is a gene amongst others
that scares fathers, concerns mothers,
while (still) gay people everywhere
crying out for them to care

No matter colour, sex or creed,
it is on love that families should feed;
(where faith a mask for hypocrisy,
religions often found guilty)

Gay people have a right to be
free of cultural prejudices and bigotry
making us feel we must defend
our sexuality to the end . . .

It's good to be open, honest, true,
but what are gay people supposed to do
when love for family put on the line,
urging us our selves to redefine?

If a faith in God fills heart and soul,
how can gay people expect to reconcile
teachings of universal love and peace
with examples holy leaders set us?

We can but follow love's golden rules,
(if made to carry its burdens like mules)
in a common humanity put our trust,
shake off its exceptions, like dust

Some will always find excuses for war,
gay and straight folks wage another?

R N Taber

For The Duration . . .

Ode To Being Single

In the morning when I wake
It's not to the sound of snoring.
I can open my curtains
I don't have to feel around in the dark
Trip over the shoes you left lying around
Or tread in your skiddy underpants.

I am free to go out when I please
Without having to say where I've been
Or who I've been with.
I can go shopping for new clothes
And I don't have to hide them
And pretend I've had them for months.

When I get back home I can listen to
Eighties music all day long if I wish.
I don't have to endure your cooking
Or the disaster area you left when you cooked it.
I don't have to ask how your day was in fact
If I don't want to talk at all . . . I won't.

In the evening I take full control of the remotes
I don't have to listen to the sound of you hyperventilating
Whenever a half-dressed woman crosses the screen
And I can have a difference of opinion
Without being called a mad man hater.

At night I have a whole double bed to myself
I don't have to put up with farting for entertainment
And endless naff jokes after the 'event'
I don't have to sneak to the bathroom to please myself
Because you couldn't manage it.
I can wear comfortable knickers
The toilet seat is always down
And I don't have to shave, in fact, if I want,
I can be as hairy as a yeti!

Carol Ann Lewis

Love Letter To Flo, My West Highland Terrier

I hope you are well Flo. Since you went away
The nights are much longer, much longer than day.
The days are all soulless, all cloudy and grey.
Do you know how I miss you since you went away?
The twelve years I knew you sped by in a trice.
We thought we had time to do everything twice
But that isn't true, Flo, life isn't that nice;
Each one of us lives by the throw of a dice.

It's frosty outside now; the nights are so cold,
As cold as my heart felt the day I was told
That you had a tumour and wouldn't grow old -
Oh, how could I lose you, more precious than gold?
An op was suggested. Where fools shouldn't tread
My family and I by the surgeons were led
But it just didn't work Flo, and I held your head
And three seconds later I knew you were dead.

The doctors were sorry. They said they had tried
To pick out your cancer and oh, how I cried
But my sad, lonely loss has been Heaven's good gain
And at least you no longer have illness and pain.
What happened to you, Flo, will burn me for years.
The fire won't diminish; the future it sears
But the flames won't be able to dry all my tears
Now I can't see your face and I can't scratch your ears.

I look to the future, the future's all black.
I wish I could have my dear terrier back.
She was the centre, the boss of our pack.
Now I've only her ashes and a little brass plaque.
She was bossy and raucous and, oh, such a friend
But what an ignoble and terrible end
For such a companion and I feel remorse
At trying to halt her immutable course

5 years on
I'm thinking about her as I drink my tea.
Our summers in Norfolk and her in the sea.

She loved all the wavelets. Our lives were so free.
Though I'd love to go back there it never can be
And I lift up my cup in salute even though
My heart bleeds each time that I turn the knife slow -
But on odd occasions my memory will glow
And there she is, *happy*, my beautiful *Flo*.

Lesley S Robinson

All In The Mind

Can we do it now love?
Are you as keen as I?
Your mother's in the garden
You know how time will fly.

We did it in the wardrobe
We did it in the sink
Oh my, that was a hasty one
You're looking rather pink.

Can we do it now love?
Are you as keen as I?
Your father's in the wardrobe
Your mother's standing by.

They saw us in the coal shed
They saw us in the snow
(Not a very pretty sight)
But now they want a go.

Margaret Swan

The Date

I went to meet a person on a date
Something we have all done and can relate
Worn roses on our chests
Carried books, papers and most things of interest
Organised that special place to meet
Excited but nervous on the way to greet
Doubt of what to find in that meeting place
Heart thumping at the arrival of what you face
There you stand, lost and forlorn
Wishing that you had never been born
People passing to and fro
Backwards and forwards in the confusion they go
And there she stands with rose in hand
Six foot eight and twenty stone and not was planned
And you think to yourself in panic, *is she the one?*
Rose screwed up and gone
As she reaches for her mobile phone
And she dials; you are on your own
Waiting for your phone to ring
And deep down wanting to smash the thing
If it rings there's nowhere to hide
Excuses and you want to scream inside
It can't be me, please it can't be me
But the realisation it's not my phone ringing you see
And there's the victim on his phone, they meet and say hello
Shake each other's hands and off they blow
Breathing a sigh of relief now they have gone
And thinking, *wasn't I the lucky one*
What about my date you ask, how did it go?
As per usual they didn't show.

Terry J Powell

A Second Chance

It started with a word, a smile
Then conversation for a while.
Friendship with a cup of tea
Empathy between him and me.

We talked of our loves who'd gone
From this, their earthly place, too long
We felt so very much alone,
Now they no longer shared our home.

But then we found that we had hope
With sharing thoughts then we could cope.
But often tears fell like stormy rain
Sometimes we managed to laugh again.

It seemed our past loves were not lost
The river of tears was finally crossed,
Memories grew and found their place
In happy times they'd shared life's race.

Our lives were strengthened and then we knew
We could mend our broken hearts, with loving too
Once again we were filled with joy and fun
We wanted to share and stay as one.

If those in Heaven hear our voice we say
Thank you for giving us our love today.
The sun shines in our souls once more
Now we'll walk on through life's open door.

Barbara Blackston

The Wings Of Love

The long, dark days of winter
Make our spirit low
Yet the birds are singing
We see flowers grow.

Reminding us of God's great love
Whate'er the days may bring
We are all God's creatures
Sheltered by His wings.

God knows and understands
The fears, in silence and alone
Nothing we experience
Our Saviour hasn't known.

The wings of love o'ershadow us
Lightening all our fears
Guiding and uplifting
Especially through tears.

'Tis then we feel His presence
As we trust Him for each hour
Remembering all God's creatures
Live by His power.

The calm and peace of blessing
Is given from above
As we thank and praise Him
For o'ershadowing wings of love.

Elva Knott

Withered Rose Of Love

Love is like a beautiful flower
It grows within the heart,
The bloom in mine, over time
Sadly falls apart.
Petals float and wither away
Upon a stream of tears,
Every hope, every wish
Drowned in passing years.
So sings a thousand love songs
But no one takes the stage,
So sings a thousand love songs
Trapped within a cage,
One tiny little lovebird
Precious as she sings,
One tiny little lovebird
That cannot spread her wings.
How can life be so cruel
To imprison all that's right,
Allow love to fade away
Like shadows in the night?
So much love within my heart
Its perfume barely traced,
A faint aroma that's disappeared
From where it was once placed.
Deep within a delicate flower
Its colour crimson-red
A beautiful rose that bathed in love
But now that love is dead.

Lisa Jane Mills

Unwrapped

As dawn breaks, passionate sound of singing birds
opening my mind looking at my lady of desire asleep
under my cover of love with her gorgeous seducing eyes of kindness

From the past haunting the anguish from my heart
some days my memories are enlightened with a slow decaying
picture of beautiful thoughts remembering you

Sinking beneath this unwrapped love of romance enticing her soul
towards my spinning web of entangled dreams
catching those magical moments as time never stands still

Linking my thoughts with my eyes of many suggestions
telling my stories from my soul of history
those treasured moments stand still in my memory of you

Clear skies above this monument of ageing beauty
thinking with my heart of satisfying, pleasing
that encouraging curse we all call love

Enticing that desire to feel my heart-throbbing wow you gave me
when you appear so transparent yet so elegant
that appealing affection you bring out of me

Remembering those souls who care for you in many different ways
are tinted stars of the night.

Paul Thackeray

Commitment

I need your love each moment I'm awake
And in my sleep I need to know you're there.
I need to feel your hand held firmly into mine
And know you'll be beside me for all time.
I need to feel the blanket of your love
Wrapping around me, keeping me from harm.
When birds no longer fly above
Then I need your love to keep me warm.
I want you as the day draws to its close.
When animals lie snugly in their lairs.
When dusk turns into twilight I need you most
For when you hold me close I lose my cares.
Each season of the year I need your love.
In May's fresh springtime or summer's sizzling heat.
When November's leaves come tumbling from above
Or winter's ice crackles 'neath my feet.
And in the darkness of the shades of night
To have you near turns my darkness into light.
In the sun's golden glow I have need of you
For then I can look into your eyes and I can see
That as much as I have need of you - so you need me.

Pamela Matthews

If I Could Reach You Any Time I Feel Like . . .

And talk to you like the way before
I am sure
You must be wishing the same too
But cannot do so even if you want to
Life is too harsh and insecure for you.
I know, you cannot share the secret
Of your thoughts, you may fret
At the responsibilities that are set
For us in this vicious circle
Entangling us at all times and all level;
You know how I feel about you,
But do you believe now?
Would you come to see me?
But you have other things to view.
The sick and ill, all need you
More than I do!
Wherever I may be, why should you worry?
Our ways were not the same, so sorry -
If I could reach you I would tell you
How much I think of you
How much your vision appears
And disappears,
How much I weep and keep
A smiling face before other tears
Stream down silently and I
Ask myself - why did I meet you, in life -
If I could reach you I would perhaps ask
You may have the answer to -
Why people have fears?
If I could reach you
I may get the peace that I got before
From you and thought it would stay
But nothing is forever,
But why do we miss people and think of them
Even if they do not wish to be remembered?
If I could reach you I would tell you
That it was something in your eyes

And your affectionate smiles
The two things that bring people close
And I called you like 'A Rose' -
If I could reach you I would tell you
You take my time and thoughts still
Even if you are away for miles and miles.

Anjum Wasim Dar

Strangers

I invited to bear with me
But not confided my theft. Strangely
The flame consumed your innocence
And charred me to death.

With each breath you uncoiled, unveiled
From the cocoon as if the alien had compromised
The barrier screen. You emerged from
An artefact to a mysterious journey of being.

The frenzy spikes of your emotions
Bevelled the edges of my patience
Yet I lay still. Made it utmost for you
As the incredulous moments passed by.

Unrecorded, unnoticed; each clamped
In other's arm in ecstasy. When we parted
We'd no regrets, we knew nothing about
The past, the present, so overwhelming.

Soumyen Maitra

Love Defined

Love is a wondrous thing
Two people, eyes meet
They glow with light
Stare, glare
With charm
Chemistry released
Sense of smell, potent
Heart beats faster
Then,
No longer master
Feelings within
Like a whirl round and round
Listen
You don't hear a sound
You both cherish that moment
Serene, complex
Bodies on fire
Lips are pouched
Rosy cheeks, flushed to the brim
Body sweats
Dripping
Regenerating again
This moment of love
Destiny prevails
Your soulmate's here
Lust
Follows with cheer
That twinkle in your eyes
Proves wonderful things
The irony of love, gives life
Love, at first sight
Can happen, in one night
One moment
Oh divine love
My heart is aching
For your touch
First kiss
Love you so much
We devour

For The Duration . . .

Like bees in a flower
This wonderful day
Should be cherished
Go on and flourish
With offspring to enfold
Life's wonder to hold
Time passing the years
Life's adheres
Love shines through
Cos it's so true
Remembering that day
Eyes meet
Vision see
Not aware, how you gleam
Memories forever
You will hold,
Your story, won't be told
Cos love is private
Through and through
My darling
I love you.

Helen Vesey

Red Lily

In the cage of my heart a lily blooms,
Scarlet petals fall in an empty room,
A morning star disappears . . .
'Another day without you.'

Margaret Pedley

Dear Love

You have been gone a year,
Filling me with great sadness.
I can no longer reach you here,
In times of gladness.
Little things would please you so, just
Have to let them go.
Always hoping that you would know.
There are times when I feel your presence near,
Brings a smile, then a tear.
Such a heartbreaking pain,
Wishing you were back again.
Just want you to guide me,
With your loving hands,
As life's problems come around,
Always seem more,
When one is down.
Sometimes I'm feeling brave, can
Face anything,
Then it hits me, you are not there.
Feel like a bird,
With only one wing.
I'm sometimes sad,
Seeing you again, would make me feel glad.
Wanting to go to bed with you,
Feel your arms, so safe around me,
Keeping all bad things away,
Which you would have me treat so lightly.
Touch my face, with your guiding hand,
Leading me to your wonderful land,
Where there is no pain or sadness,
Only our love, so full of gladness.
For the moment,
Please be a bright and twinkling star,
For me, my Mr Man
Then I will join you, when I can.

Your Deb.

Mabel (Deb) Moore

Love You

The sunshine's all around your grace
Keeping everything in place
Just seeing you is such a joy
A heart of gold! Yes I'd employ
To help me out in so many ways
I really hope that this love stays
Be it money or honey - you are mine
And true love forever will be divine
Yet I have to tell you a story
All my family is a personal glory
I love all of you that stand in line
And to you my wife - you are so divine
So enjoy each day - you delightful girl
With a love and grace! You diamond pearl.

Lee Connor

Together Forever

I thought our love was forever
But we soon fell apart,
I found out you were married
And you just broke my heart.

You always brought me flowers
But flowers don't hide the pain,
They only make it hurt worse
As you look at them again and again.

I went out with your best friend
After years we're still together,
We've got married now
And our love will go on forever.

Trudie Sullivan

Unison

The bride was breathtakingly beautiful
in a black designer dress
a tiara on her dark hair
jewellery to match.
She looked as though she stepped
from the catwalks of Paris or Milan.

The groom was tall and handsome,
dressed in grey
with a large tattoo on his wrist,
his hair cut in an alternate style
shaved at the sides, brushed at the top.

It was a love affair from the start
as surrounded by family and friends
they made their commitment
in a beautiful church on the outskirts.

Their baby lay gurgling in its pram
full of the joys of life
as everyone headed for the reception
in a sumptuous house
that catered for weddings, parties
meals or B&B.

A rock band was playing,
fantastic was the word
heard throughout the evening.

Everyone said they had
a marvellous time
and did not want it to end.
But then when you think about it
this was a 21st century romance,
in the year 2009.

Rosaleen Clarke

For The Duration . . .

A Little Thought

A little thought I sent away,
One cold winter's day;
A little thought just meant for you,
To bring you joy and happiness thru'.

Time passed on and new years came,
Alone I remained in silent requiem;
I searched you here, I searched you there,
I searched you everywhere.

Nowhere in sight, yet you were there,
In my heart, too close to part;
I rekindled a burning desire
Which lit my soul, consumed me entire.

A distant light I saw in vain,
Your ethereal figure rising up the plain;
Faster and faster swung the pendulum of time,
I knew you could no longer be mine.

My eyes turned hazy, my tears were dead,
I could see no path to tread;
Faceless were you to me then,
Hopeless was hope to me.

Shamim Ruhi

Grandmothers

Grandmothers love kisses whether from a babe or a grown man
They value them like precious stones and collect them
                                              when they can.
Hugs are also welcome, the longer they last the better
They make them feel wanted again and close to
                                              what they treasure.
Have you given a kiss or hug to someone living on their own?
One day you will realise what I mean, if you are all alone.

Audrey Faulkner O'Connor

Only One
(For Annie . . .)

It is only at night, when the stars come out, that I have
                                               time to think.
I lie, gleaming moonlight and spectacles of dust looking over me.
I watch as the last candle is extinguished.
The world is asleep now, but this is my time.

My mind takes me on a journey, a mystery trip.
We venture far and wide.
Where do we go each night?
Anywhere.
The silence is majestic, so I lay in awe.

I sometimes wonder about my life, how I would have
                                             done things differently.
Prevented bad habits before they began, worked harder at school.
So many needless errors.
Oh how my life would be different if I could turn back the clock.

Thinking back, I remember all the mistakes I've made,
And I wonder what life would be like now.
What if I could change things?
Funny though,
There is only one thing that I would never change.
That's the day I met you.

J R Parkinson

Hope Springs . . .

We haven't spoken yet
Only swapped the odd glance
Which may or may not begret
Some kind of romance
But tonight I celebrated with a drink
Because you smiled at me (I think).

M G Sherlock

For The Duration . . .

Husband - The River Of Love

Dear Husband, my love did not come as a raging torrent,
But as a silver trickling stream
Flowing from the bosom of the earth.

Meeting in its progress the rocks and boulders of life.
Trapped awhile before finding its way -
Eddying into tranquil pools, and resting there to gather strength.

Sometimes it faltered
And had to find its way,
Gently winding between the obstacles of human living.

But it grew strong and deep
Carrying the seeds of life in its silent progress,
To become a love so wide and powerful
That only an ocean could absorb its greatness.

Ann Dempsey

My Husband, My Pal

My best friend, I met some time ago
I tell all my secrets, his face it never shows
A gentle and most kinder friend
His heart is the biggest I could never comprehend
We share a love that grows stronger day by day
Money is always in short supply
Gifts and presents do not bother me
His love is the greatest gift, all can see
The world is an oyster of a greater lovely gift
This man he gives me love they try to shift
Keep all the jewels that much wealth they give
We take our love, and show how to live
All to see his pain he tries to show me
This love is ours for the world to see
He is my lover, my pal and my husband
We show our love to this unhappy land.

Yvonne Stevens

Gillian - A Love Cry

In the surgery,
Ella Fitzgerald comes on the intercom:
'Every time you say goodbye
I die a little; through major or
Minor: and - through old Manhattan
Through old Manhattan and the
Bronx . . .'

Then I see you Doc,
As you hold my face
In your sweet hands,
And comfort me.
I cannot help loving you;
You resemble my own,
My dearest darling Gillian,
Whom I cannot see -
Not forever, Lord -
Please not forever,
Jesus hear me,
Not forever.

I go home, a thoroughly mixed-up lad,
And say the rosary. Don't let illness
Carry me off Lord, not till I've written
My epic works, and helped
All mankind, man and woman.

Young teenage girls pass
My window, and gorsh, humorous youths.
God how I feel sorry for them -
They are unemployed, hardened
To street violence and crime,
And suckers for VD.

Help them as well as the doctor Lord,
Let them have something good to live for.

Angie; Angie; you are
In authority over me, my 'care co-ordinator'
For my schizophrenia. Work with me,
Not against me - you have saved my life
Many times this past six months.

And so I pray for all people,
High and low, good and bad,
Male and female.
'Man must have his mate,
That you cannot deny'.

Gillian, I made a love cry:
I will gladden your heart with children,
My chevy, my only one,
Only come to me now,
Before it is too late,
And the ravages of time
Take their bite.

You are tall, pretty of face,
Slim and long in the leg,
Not a sex bomb - they have
All the men after them;
But a good plain girl,
Who knows what she loves,
And loves what she knows.

Your kisses are so sweet,
Your lips like perfumed velvet,
You draw my coat about you,
It is winter now, and you feel
The cold . . . you are epileptic,
Poor sad kid.

And I am schizophrenic.
Cure us both, dear Jesus,
And give us a triumphant
Wedding, with friends,
Lots of flowers - real irises
For your headdress,
And a long white gown.

Pretty little bridesmaids,
And I carry you over
The threshold . . .

A fortnight in Paris, and
The ecstasy of consummation,
My darling, my only one.

R O'Shaughnessy

Doves

Hands, like doves, flutter;
Leave their shadow on my heart.
Fingers, soft wing tips, caress,
Tingle, nerves break and part.

Feather-strokes smooth my limbs
Swoop in unexpected arcs.
Perch, settle, scratch my thighs
Prickle, tickle, leave delicate marks.

Dancing, cooing, drumming
Feathers, claws and beaks
Lift and rise, in urgent clutching
Carry me soaring to faraway peaks.

Turning, I trap them
Those doves, now becalmed
To rest, to dream, to brood
Come to nest in the shade of my heart.

Tessa Paul

Journey To The East

Rebirth for love
Reunited with true self
No longer poor in spirit
I had eternal wealth
Reawakened heart
An inner glow
Releases a natural flow
Our souls to mate
Remembered memories run parallel
A journey far
To relight me
I lost what I needed
Becoming receded
For a precious moment
She revealed the love in me.

Louis Cecile

True Love

Lovers kiss
Beneath the trees,
That are blowing gently
In the breeze,
They always say farewell
But never goodbye,
Because true love
Stays together,
Until they die.

Sylvia Wynne

Just To Tell You

Audrey, my love for you is endless
How other could it be, when you are in my vision?
With everything I see
My heart is full to bursting with my endless thoughts of you,
You are lovely and I love you so what else can I do?

I love the times we have together,
The simple things we do, the quiet times,
The happy times when I am close to you,
I love the smiles you give me, the wave that's in your hair,
Your thoughtfulness, your company, the simple way you care.

So Audrey, I can't help it as the days go drifting by
That I pray for time together, that time for you and I.
To deepen our friendship, so much time that has been lost
Can never be recaptured, no matter what the cost,
So what we have we must hold tight and never let it go
And let the peace that's with us shed a warm and cosy glow.

Cyril G Payne

My Husband

Your lips touch mine, I tremble.
My body seems to ache
For that rich embrace you give me
Every time I awake.
You tell me that you love me every passing day
My tower of strength to help me
Along life's rocky way.
We'll both grow old together
Which makes me want to say
That I love you too my darling
I know that I am sure
That our love will last forever
Until there is no more.

Margaret Kent

The New Spirituality

What you really believe
You think, you say and you do
Are 'the energies' you create
That will make up 'the real you'

So follow this simple formula
In your every day to day
Based on, and motivated by 'love'
In 'the new spirituality' way

For if we believe in 'love'
And try to think most loving thoughts
Then this is the best way forward
That now needs to be fervently sought

If you speak words of kindness
Support, caring and 'love'
Then you will be much applauded
By all of those, way 'up above'

If your personal actions are honourable
Whilst thinking of others besides
Then you will 'journey' gently onward
To where your 'real self' over-rides

That 'self being' that is of 'love'
Creating 'the light' deep down inside
A 'special space' of joy, calm and peace
Where your 'soul' does quietly abide

This is 'the new spirituality'
Really quite easy you can see
Create in yourself, 'a being of love'
Then reflect this 'light', for others to see

If we could all take responsibility
And try hard to create all of this
Then 'ourselves' and 'the world' would experience
A long, loving state, of pure and joyous bliss.

Jade Deacon

Our Daughter's 18th Birthday

Our lifetime is a journey on a long and winding road
Some paths are marked quite clearly
And some are almost obscured
The journey would be easy if we could always read all the signs
But sadly we often stumble and the sun doesn't always shine
Today is another milestone on your journey through this life
And I prayed for brilliant sunshine to bathe you in its light
I remember the other milestone the day you first went to school
You were beautiful, bright and eager
But then you always were as a rule
It was lovely to see you so happy on that very special day
I remember that sudden lost feeling and I cried as I came away
Today is your eighteenth birthday,
The pathways you choose are your own
New people, new places, new friendships,
Now into an adult you have grown
Sometimes the pathways are hilly
And the upward road seems so long
When your struggle seems to be hardest
Stride out for the top with a song
The view from the top is quite thrilling
As you look on ahead and beyond
The future always holds promise
And is worth waiting for I have found
So when you are footsore and weary
Just remember the view from the top
And take each day a few minutes
To count all the blessings you've got
Your days will be filled with laughter,
Your heart will be filled with love
Bright moonlight nights and sweet kisses
Are just some of the things you will have
I say all this quite truly and I know it is still all to come
But everyone should have them
And I'm sure you will find some

I'm proud of you at this milestone
And I look forward to each new one you find
May they all mark your way to be happy
And thoughtful and loving and kind.

Milly Holme

Love

I tell you that I love you,
In many, many ways,
In little deeds and gestures,
Not often in big displays.

I show you that I love you,
When you are feeling low,
I put my arms around you,
Just to let you feel I know

That we all need love within our lives,
It makes the world go round,
It's the strangest felt emotion,
That ever has been found.

Just to love and be loved in return
Is more precious than jewels or gold,
It's been there since the start of life,
It's ours to have and hold.

You do not need to have money
To give love or receive,
It's a universal language,
It's what we should believe.

If you love someone and are loved in return
You are truly, richly blessed,
You can cope with life, tackle any strife,
And let life take care of the rest.

Edna Rudge

First Love

Where did you go to my first love
From all those years ago
The one who set my heart alight
The first time I saw you?
I will always remember that first night
I walked into a room and saw you sitting there
I didn't know who you were
But I fell in love right there
I could not get you off my mind
You lit up my heart
I had never been in love before
I didn't know where to start
You spoke to me and asked me out
My nerves were all a-flutter
I said yes without a doubt
But said it with a stutter
A few days later the time had come
For our very first date
I got ready with so much excitement
I didn't want to be late
You took me to the cinema
You held my hand so tight
And at the end of the evening
You kissed me tenderly and said goodnight
We shared so many times like that
Together you and I
Then something started going wrong
Instead of pulling together we just couldn't get along
The love which had brought us together
Suddenly fizzled out
I do still think about you
Now all those years have passed us by
I wonder if you got married
What you did with your life
Do you ever think of me the way I think of you?
The one I fell in love with first all those years ago.

Janet Thomas

Loss
(For Steve, the love of my life - 1951-2006)

Every day is a grey day
Even when the sky is blue
Every day is a lonely day
Because I don't have you.

The birds don't sing at break of day
Even though it's spring
The joyous season of rebirth
No longer means a thing.

The summer sun has lost its glow
The tides still ebb and flow
Life goes on regardless
How I just don't know.

Autumn brings the fall of leaf
The howling winds and rain
And I would just give anything
To have you back again.

They say time is a healer
And that may well be true
But for me time's standing still
As all I want is you.

Margaret Martin

Tapestry

You are the tapestry of my life,
Your threads hold me together,
Your colour gives me happiness,
Each stitch to give no one else but you.
Uniqueness, completeness,
Blissfulness, peacefulness,
Never to be unwoven,
Nor unravelled past the end of time.

Isabel Taylor

Daffodils In The Snow

Daffodils in the snow remind me of that springtime long ago
When love was warm and I was all wrapped up in you
How we loved, how we laughed in that cottage in the snow
Using the day's newspapers to try and make the coal fire go
Giving up and lying on the floor in a heap
Laughing and loving and falling asleep
Raiding the cupboards, ravenous for food
Running out of coal and searching for wood
No milk for tea, I gave it all to the cat
A sliced-up orange in the cup, a new taste sensation,
Yes, I like it like that
Washing the dishes, cooking the food
I never knew life could be this simple and this good
Two people in a world full of love
The snow falling softly from the heavens above
'I love you very much,' you said
'I've always loved you,' you said
'I miss you,' you said
I tried to think, not with my heart but with my head
Failed and fell hopelessly under love's spell
I thought you had as well
The crocuses, the early daffodils
A golden glow, peeping through the snow
How could you have Irish eyes?
So blue and sparkling just like my grandpa's so I'm told?
How could you be so warm and then so cold?
How could you leave, how could you go?
When the warm spring sun began to melt the snow and you
Turning away in the space of a day
From lover to leaver
Why did you go?
What did you know then that I didn't know?
You arrived with armfuls of flowers and a February valentine
I thought, *at last, at last, he's really all mine*
How could you leave me here in tears
After all those places
All those faces, all those loving years?
We laughed and cried in the sun and the rain
And we glowed in the snow

'I love the way you laugh,' you said
'It makes me laugh,' you said
'When you cry you are even more beautiful,' you said
I'm on the train now, in the snow
Going to the same place we went to long ago
The daffodils are peeping through
My every thought is still of you
It's not the same without you
It never can be
The daffodils in the snow are still the same as long ago
But I wish you were here to see
That without you, I'm not the same me.

Dorothy Ellen Connor

Is This A Dream?

I was just getting used to yesterday
When along came today.
Crashing into my life you came.
Now everything is upside down and will never be the same.

Your head and mine filled with beautiful dreams.
Bright new, brand new, hopeful schemes.
Each of us a half, a whole, a mind, a soul, a heart.
The growing day by day, never wanting to be apart.

Sweet-smelling flowers and powder-blue skies.
Hearts beating together as one, entwined are we.
With the light of loving in our eyes.

Both aware of our love for each other so strong.
But is this a dream
Or is it where we belong?

Sheila Richford

Undercover Conversations

She lays open, but closed, only covered by the red silk bed sheet.
Stroking the invisible lines, from which I intend to repeat.
Involuntary footsteps, brown eyes, soft hands, perfect breasts.
Whispers of desire, surf the air between her mouth and my ear.
Rotation, embrace, no more is she covered.

With a gentle touch of tongue on skin, of pink,
Breathe not, as she tenses in deep red.
We subliminally transmit pre-scripted natures,
As she phonetically undresses my surface.
As she bites her lips, instructing movements, maximising sensation.
Effortless intertwining, embodies our structural connection.
From which I assure her ascent.

The sapphire night shines upon our crimson flame.
As we curtain ourselves under deep red,
Utilising every corner, direction and angle, our movements spread.
Velocity at which she moves increased, as she gazes upon me.
Tense tight, eyes white, as screams for an arrest in our actions.
My enlightened mind travels as it advocates for more passion.

Her body no more, as she drips to her core
Her satisfaction conveyed by reactions.
Embraced under daylight, under God's eye.

This was the love shared between a man and his wife.

Mahadi Kyeyune

Further

The delicate handcrafted carvings of the fireplace were chipped,
And the coal fire's warmth still dispersed around the room.
The Victorian coving cracked at the edges, leaking down
                                    the damp walls.
Soot lined the chimney, where the depth of your cry used to echo.

It was here that our skin felt the air between our bodies.
The canopy bed shifted 3 inches left from where we left it,
Moth-eaten curtains hung off the columns.
Dust clung to my clothes, as though I had been enraptured
                                    by the room.

In the midst of reality I could feel the arch of her back
                        in my hand once again.
The way that our faces would reflect each other's -
Now the mirror yearns for a fresh face to paint.

The smell of 56 years still sits in the furniture;
The windows were stiff and unopened.
The blinds shuttered whilst the red night sky set.

Feeling a weakness in the wooden floor, beneath my feet,
It began to give way.
Closing the door with its brass handle;
The banister of the stairway collapsed at the grip of my hand.

Melissa Brabanski

Dear God

Dear God,
Please make me a man,
Who is kind and gentle, but also if you can,
Make him good-looking, just like Thomas Magnum,
Dark, tall, hairy and full of wicked fun.
Dress him in the finest that Armani can create,
Smother him with 'Eternity' to put me in a state.
Oh, don't forget the music, a little touch will do,
Of Chopin, Pavarotti, Elvis, David Essex too.
He needs to be a dancer of versatile techniques,
Ballet, Latin, disco, to dance me off my feet.
I'd really like a sailor, who's travelled on the seas,
Who wants to take me places and is willing to please.
If you could possibly manage an extra ingredient,
With this lover that is Heaven-sent.
Amen.

V Fitzpatrick

My Love

Does my love, love me?
He never tells me so
Does my love, love me?
He sure let's me know

I'll-health floored me for a spell
My love came to the fore
He washed me, he fed me
Cooked, cleaned and more

Forty-four years we're wed
I thank God for him
I would have laid down and died
Without his love.

Rachel Ritchie

For The Duration . . .

Love Of Life

Is there such a thing as life without love?
Take a good look at the Earth and the sky up above.
The merry bright colours, the gay laughing crowds.
The quick change of weather and the soft dancing clouds.

No matter what the weather, rain, sleet or sun,
Life can still be a pleasure and many things be done.
To walk along a sandy lane, picking plants and seeds
Or walk along a sandy shore, or wherever your trail leads.

Wherever you may go love is always to be seen,
Among the tiny animals playing in the evergreen.
With children walking hand in hand, no bitterness between
And black and white together, on each the other lean.

Rosie Hues

The Windmill

When taken by the wind
it comes to life, says - yes!
*Your hair did that too
at the top of Meldon Hill.*

On gentle days it dreams,
ponders all that space,
*like you when we stood that day
high up on Hamel Down.*

When slow clouds drift
it takes time off from work.
*Under drifting clouds
we took time off too.*

Christopher Highton

Looking Back In My Mind

Decisions made back in the past,
I thought were for the best,
But looking back, I see these plans
Caused heartache and regret.

When you were very young and small
I chose to marry, be a wife.
I never thought about the risk
Of damaging your life.

You were the first born of my children,
I never meant to cause you pain
I've loved you as much as the others
And tried to treat you all the same.

I thought that I was doing right,
But I know I was a fool,
I didn't want to change your life
Make new friends and start new school.

I left you with my parents
Each weekend you'd come to stay
You made a fuss when time to go
You wanted to stay here and play.

In time, I had your brother,
You must have felt left out,
Then soon I had your sister,
Your young mind was full of doubt.

My family told you stories
Of how I didn't care,
Of how my love had vanished
And I wanted just the younger pair.

I may not have been right by your side,
But I've not been far away.
You've always been here in my heart
And that's where you'll always stay.

For The Duration . . .

You moved across the water
But not so very far
We keep in touch by phone and mail,
At least I know just where you are

It's taken up so many years
To find again, each other's heart
And now I want the world to know
We never more will part.

Farina May Jenkins

A Box Filled With You

May I keep my precious thoughts of you,
Inside a crystal box.
Hidden well in a special place,
Secured with many locks.

I will keep it safe and close to hand,
Should I ever feel blue,
I shall open up my crystal box,
And surround myself with thoughts of you.

The closeness that we once had shared,
The warmth you offered me,
To feel your arms around my soul,
In a place I dreamt I'd never be.

But the gift of time was not that of ours,
Our souls untwined, no longer one,
Yet I will always have my crystal box,
And my thoughts of you, although you're gone.

Sharon Reed

For My Love

My thoughts are acting wildly as though they've taken wing
My heart is beating madly, oh if only it could sing
Rainbows dance before me spinning colours on a thread
Orchestras play love songs here inside my head.

This man you see before you only lives when you are near
I'm a shell, an empty vessel, a cry without a tear
My senses lying dormant like shadows in the night
Then you approach, I feel you near, my fears are put to flight.

I now see very clearly which direction I must take
Your influence a guideline to each movement that I make
For you are my love, my friend and my life
You're the girl I am planning to take for my wife.

Now you are here beside me and as I hold your hand
I've never felt so humble, yet how proudly I stand
You are my beloved, all I'll ever need
So now I hand with love to you the emotions you have freed.

M W Grainger

Memories

Your memories are like shadows of the night.
An emptiness that cannot be filled
No one can wipe away the tears of yesterday
Your love is a seed blown on the wind
Although we can never be together
We will never be apart.

Pamela Javes

For The Duration . . .

First Love

There were no primroses, tinted with sun by thorn-bound hedgerow.
No birds piped their tune in shimmering elms.
Only a rusting shunt-engine clanked its hollow tattoo,
Breaking the velvet stillness of the chill November night.
No magic touched the oil-dark waters of the brooding city river;
Save for the factory windows mirrored nervously
Beyond the metal bridge.
A swan, homing late, whispered its way behind a tethered barge.
The girl beside me stopped to watch.
Caught in the pale glow of the slumbering city,
Her smile rang in my heart.
Gently, warm in the winter frost, we kissed.

The artlessness of youth could never hope to reap
The glowing promise of that second's bliss.
Warm eyes, cool lips and oh! that shining hair.

Soon she was gone.
Only a memory remains, as fresh as yesterday,
Of that far moment's breathless, yet exquisite pain.
Darkness embraced the silent echo of our meeting lips
Sending it flying far into the starlit vaults of space.
Somewhere, I think, it lingers still
To mock the passing of the hurrying years,
Witness 'til the twilight of the world
That once, on a soft November night,
I held my first love in my wondering arms
And knew the infinite envy of the ageless gods.

David Ryan

Love's First Thoughts

Your smiling eyes
Your smiling lips
Your tender loving fingertips

Your warm caress
Your sincere kindness
Your sweet-tasting kiss

Your caring ways
Your voice that says
You're longing for my touch

You're in my thoughts
You're in my heart

I love you very much.

Paul A Taylor

I Will Sing To Her Soul

I will sing to her soul
When it ceases to sing

I will summon the song
When her heart but gives in

Will prevent one last sob
Till her mind wakes to be

And if under her breast
Her soul blazoned once more

I'll succumb having held
Its harmony no more

Yet when the blaze withers
When her heart seem'd too lost

I will sing to her soul
I will sing till it stops.

Layla Hendow

True Love

Our meeting was fulfilment of a dream, but sensed affection,
which grew stronger, still, as time passed by.

The happiness we knew swelled up to fill each atom of our space,
our marriage was a closing of the space, we

Talked of our plans and hopes, we promised new, one moment
while the universe stood still and held its breath,
we consummated love. No hunt could touch us for our new love,

Reach further than bond of time and space, which we took our
minds and increase still as time moved on. No moment could be

Still. Are unoccupied by any thought of dream, I cling to the rock
of every vow and pray time has not changed our love. I think

Of plucking peaches from the tree. I come to you with little but
my heart, determined to put rank before true love, I pray we will

Not have to live apart and sing as prayers are heard. For embrace
because I feel that in Heaven above.

Imogene Lindo

Untitled

Pretty little roses as she poses for me,
lips so smooth and full, wishing she'd
pull me closer and whisper sweet nothings
because they mean something to me.
Is it possible that she could make life worth living?
Giving me goose pimples with her dimples,
so sweet sugar tastes sour.
She gives me the power to move mountains like peas,
or sail the seas with nothing but a paddle and love.

Umer Sharif

George's Girl

George is his name
And loving me is his game,
My name is Sara Jane.

He came into my life
And made me his wife.

The love he has for me
Is far greater than I can believe.

He's loving and caring,
Giving and sharing.

But most of all, he thinks the world of me,
For his love is ever growing,
As far as the eye can see.

Sara Jane Berry

You Are The One

You are the one I'll forever adore
You are the one my love is for.
One glance at you and my heart quickens pace
Even in dreams I see your dear face.

You are the one who can change my complexion
You are the one who holds all my affection.
You're with me on waking and with me on sleeping
My life and my love I place in your keeping.

You are the one who can thrill me my dear
You are the one who I love to have near.
When we are together it is heaven for me
Held close in your arms, no one could happier be.

You are the one for whom I'll keep a date
You are the one for whom I always will wait.
You live in my heart each night and each day
I love you my darling and will do for aye.

Esther Hawkins

There Can Be Only One

I don't know where or how to start
To tell the tale of a captured heart,
This heart was mine, or so I thought
The love inside could not be bought.

Then you came along and cast a glance
It was love at first sight, yes true romance,
At thirteen years old I was barely a teen
You were the most beautiful girl I had ever seen.

We were only kids, a shy boy and a girl
Yet you made me dizzy, had my head in a whirl,
I didn't know the meaning of love or desire
How you turned me on, setting my soul on fire.

From that moment of magic, that unforgettable first kiss
You made me feel so special, you made my life bliss,
With my hand on my heart I can honestly say
I have never looked at another girl in the same way.

If it takes two to tango, don't we make a pair?
You're my Ginger Rogers and I'm your Fred Astaire
The discos, the parties, all the good times and bad,
We've been through it all, sometimes happy, some sad.

We are as much in love now, as we were then
So meant to be together, just a matter of when,
Now, thirty-six years on since our marriage took place
The day you said yes put a permanent smile on my face.

Do you know? In all that time one thing's remained true
That is the never-ending love in my heart, just for you,
You have always been the girl of my dreams
Been my wife and my lover in all of my schemes.
You're the love I would die for, may we go on and on anon
I meant what I said, there can be only one, *you!*

Christopher Thomas

Precious Moments

It's only a dream.
I'm waiting for your
Love to land on me.
A secretive theme.
I'm waiting for your
Love to set me free.

I've waited so long,
And now my loneliness
Has grown so much.
My feelings are strong.
I'm waiting for a chance
To feel your touch.

A moment in time.
My heart will never
Last another day.
Is loving a crime?
I long to hear the
Tender words you say.

Just give me a call.
I'm waiting day and night
For you to phone.
My back's to the wall.
I never want to spend
Another night alone.

I'm shrouded in doubt.
I thought that you would
Feel the same for me.
I scream and shout.
I'm waiting for a chance
To finally make you see

How much that I care.
The sadness in my eyes -
They cry for you.
I'll always be there,
Believing in the love
I know is true.

Peter Steele

Chemistry

It's not who you are
Or who you've been
It's not what you look like or resemble
It's the chemistry
It's being one with the other
Husband, wife or lover
Souls entwined
It's all in the mind
And the heart
Not wanting to be apart
Our psyche is so powerful
You don't have to think
It's not even the effect of
Getting woozy after a drink
It's when two become one
Soulmates
That's true love
Chemistry!

Theresa Hartley-Mace

Jilted On My Biggest Day

We dated from our early teens
Youth club, stolen kisses, blue faded jeans
A great circle of friends as we all knocked about
Love progressing forward, no element of doubt

Moving forward, jobs on leaving school
Saving hard, occasionally bending the rules
We got engaged, money building, still great times we had
Wedding bells calling, just what could turn bad?

We found a house, and purchased the fading place
Worked like Trojans, made it our first base
Brickwork and plastering all falling out of place
Never defeated, I won the lengthy race

Everything booked, the reception, the church
What or who could knock us off our perch?
Suited and booted, the best man and me
Standing motionless, for the whole world to see

Looking at wrist watches, waiting for the car to arrive
The car vanished and so did the bride
Jilted at the altar, emotional wounds along with scars
Lying in the gutter, still reaching for the stars.

Leigh Smart

For The Duration . . .

Have You Ever . . .

Have you ever loved somebody so much it makes you want to cry?
Have you ever loved somebody so much
You miss them being by your side?

Have you ever known that you can trust that one person
With your life?
Do you always know that what they're saying is never trife?

Do you know that they would do anything for you?
Do you know that they cry when they now think of you?

Have you ever tried to convince yourself
That something so good can't be true?
Have you ever thought about it so much
It made you feel quite blue?

That person will never hurt you,
That person will never leave you.

Don't think too much
Don't shed a tear
Open your eyes and you'll see what you want
I'm right here.

I love you.

Sophie Jayne Mathews

A Kiss

A kiss on the cheek dear
I can't find you anywhere near here
A kiss on the hand
We'll act like lovers in an unpublished Shakespeare romance
A kiss in the dark
To catch you off guard like a shark in deep water
A kiss on the deck
We'll be gone with the wind like Scarlet and Rhett

If you pick the date, I'll pick the venue
We'll eat from the same old a la carte menu

A kiss on demand from a lady to a man
That's the way it is
A kiss while we stand in control and command
Feeling devilish
A kiss with a tongue that can't be undone
'Tis perfect bliss
A kiss beneath your eye against your nose as you sigh
That's my favourite kiss.

If you pick the appetiser, I'll pick the dessert
We'll kiss each other hungry until everywhere hurts

Just give me:
One kiss and I'll miss you like Cathy does Heathcliff
One kiss and I'll plummet straight into the abyss
One kiss and I'll tell you I love you then go
And then I'll kiss other people I neither love nor know.

Abigail Randall

My Rock

He is my inspiration
I have walked with him through life
We have worked together side by side
As dearest husband and wife
He is my rock, my anchor
I love him, oh so much
How would I survive, without him,
His love, his support and his touch?

There is nothing he can't do
He really is a grafter
Whatever he turns a hand to
It's a dead cert he will master
He's taught me so much about myself
Given encouragement and support
And now I'm full of a confidence
That just cannot be bought.

He's not vain, he's not conceited
He's just your average guy
No fancy clothes or showy car
No such trophies does he buy
But he thinks he is the richest man
And I have to agree,
The only treasures in his life
Are his children and me.

Denise Edmonds

You Wouldn't Know Love
If It Hit You Between The Eyes

You get through girlfriends like you get through pies
Consume and devour them like a portion of fries
They gather around you like proverbial flies
But you wouldn't know love if it hit you between the eyes

Your mind is wallpapered with breasts and thighs
Each woman is a conquest, a competition prize
You only think of one thing when your ardour starts to rise
But you wouldn't know love if it hit you between the eyes

Another weekend of alcohol highs
You're ready for the next one before the sheet dries
So what would you do if you couldn't womanise?
Cos you wouldn't know love if it hit you between the eyes

You treat your women like rugby tries
You score your points. You zip up your flies
A scrum down, a conversion and a pack of lies
But you wouldn't know love if it hit you between the eyes

It could have been 'us'. You could have been wise
But I'm just another body when you run out of supplies
So farewell to you, you b*****d! Hope your balls liquidize
Cos you wouldn't know my love, if it hit you between the eyes.

Rob Barratt

For The Duration . . .

Somehow, Some When

Somehow, some when, I know I'll try
To get through a day, when I don't cry
Somehow, some when, I'm sure to smile
At something about you, though, it'll take a while

Remembering, are the tough times
When silly little things, come to mind
Regretting every cross word, ever spoken
Treasuring every photo, that now, I try to find

To look ahead, without you
Right now, seems too hard to bear
But I know you're always near me
And I know you'll always care

Someday, somehow, some when, I *will* know
Perhaps, a day that will pass by
That instead of tears of pain and sadness
I'll be able to remember, with a sigh

Yes, somehow, some when, I know I'll try
And get through a day, without a tear to dry
Yes, somehow, some when, I know, again, that I *will* smile
At something about you, though, it'll take a while.

Shirley Sewell

What Is Life?

I felt my life had ended
When my love deserted me,
I thought I'd never smile again,
No future could I see.
I felt the years were wasted
On one who no longer cared,
For 30 years I'd loved him
With him my life I'd shared.

'Time heals,' they often told me,
But I had so many doubts,
The hurt and desperation
From my sad heart did shout.
Such love had been embedded
So deep within my heart,
I felt that I could never bear
From him to be apart.

Though at times I still feel sad,
And sometimes shed a tear,
I then remember happy times
And things that gave me cheer.
My future lies before me
It's up to me to live
And love the life God's given me
And know how to forgive.

I'm thankful for my children
Who mean the world to me,
And support from special friends -
To life they were my key.
I have so much to treasure
And to be thankful for
I have a life so full of joy
And hope, and much, much more.

Anne Gray

Summer Love In The Winter

I loved that you hid your sensitivity behind heavy metal music . . .
dark lyrics, steel and leather, the colour of night.

That metallic smell of motorbike oil and grease,
there warmth and yours, in the summertime, I recall all the more,
in the deepest dark of each winter, I pass through as I age.

For a while, you and I were all things blackest and darkest
of the winter.

The embodiment of darkness, of all things black,
our long dark hair and muted tatty, holey garb.

There was a shadow, that lay on our souls and it manifested
in our love of dark deeds, and speed and speed . . .
the rush of a short summer love, to the inevitable long winter.

Then one day you sped and sped and sped . . . away from me . . .
until you and I were no more, and I made my way to the light,
away from the winter of my soul.

Yazmin White

Shut-Eye Heaven

My heart and soul are yours to keep
As my dreams are of you in every sleep
You are my one, you are my girl
The thought of you just makes me whirl
Don't let go, hold me in tight
As me and you just feels so right.

Stuart Pickup

Valentine Lover

It's cold outside
With ice all over
It's warm in here
And in my heart
Just waiting for you
To melt the icicles
With a hug so pure
And full of love
Just for you
On Valentine's Day.

Amanda Prince

Silver Lanyards

Staring from
his own vessel
at the nape of her
neck where a lone
silver lanyard of hair
loosed towards morning -

He remembered those
voyages taken together
when night's dark sails
unfurled richer and deeper
and the stars were
out in their eyes
to navigate by one another.

Peter Asher

What Is Love?

My head spins,
My throat feels dry,
People laugh, I start to cry.
Why am I tired, yet wide awake?
Hot rushes make my body shake.
I talk too much,
I laugh too loud,
I feel alone when I'm in a crowd.
I'm with my friends
But it's not enough!
What's wrong with me?
Am I in love?

Clare Furey

Valentine Bouquet

Valentine time again
All buying their greeting cards and roses
Tulips are beautiful
Flowers also
Give me a bouquet of your tulips
To be my valentine.

Alice Collins

The Honeymoon 1935

Now what can I say after that happy wedding day?

Amy has her crocodile case packed and ready
Say a special goodbye to brother, Freddie.
Wave, wave, to all those faces -
Don't worry my darling, I'll carry the cases.

Into their MG they settled down, she wore a costume
Of chocolate brown, so slim and pretty and lovely legs.
A felt hat, soft like fudge perched on her snappy head.
And with a fond embrace they waved and waved again
And away, alone at last down the narrow lane.

They had made their haven - not Torquay,
They chose Brighton.

A quiet hotel with waitresses neat, into their bedroom
A quick retreat.

Confetti falling round their feet.
Oh, golly, golly, now they know.

Of course they'd all know without this clue
When love is fresh and excitement new.

Into their room they ventured then.
Mmm - rather good, I like the colour of the wood.
Yes, fumed oak I think it's called.

John with pressed fingers felt the bed -
'Now John,' Amy said as she sat, legs dangling on the edge,
Eiderdown feather-filled.
Oh, joy and bliss, kissey, kiss.

He picked her up and twirled her round
Her tiny feet not touching the ground.

I love you, I love you, and you're all mine.
Let's go for a walk along the Chine.
Yes, let's do that and then it will be nearly time for us to dine.

They strolled along hand in hand,
Passed the Victorian ornate bandstand.

The air was salty, the sea rolled in.
The seagulls wailed and deckchairs blew.

For The Duration . . .

Oh what bliss, kissey, kiss, kiss.

This Heaven they knew.

The sandcastles died as the sea lapped their side
Where children had played, now no more
On this quiet, calm sandy shore.

They dined together on linen white.
The waiter with a lavish sweep poured the wine for Sir
To taste - an impish grin shone on Amy's face.

Retire into another room, comfy chairs and standard lamps
Wall lights with crimson shades and patterned carpet.
A smell of nicotine -
And on a tray a pot of coffee with caffeine.

'Darling, darling, let's go to bed,' John with a whisper said.

The maid on the bed her nightie had laid
And corner of covers turned down.
The sash window slightly open,
Rumbling trams into town.

His strong arms held her tight.
My dearest love, my sweetest, sweetest turtle dove.

Warm and at peace, their arms entwined
Completely relaxed and with quiet mind.
The love, and the slumber, the nearness too.

They woke in the morning to misty dew.
Perfect, perfect bliss, kissey, kiss, kiss.

I'll love you forever in this world and the next
Come on my sweet let's have breakfast –
And then on the pier, my dearest, dearest, dear.

Poppy Gooday

Yolanda Scores

Yolanda
met Miranda
and didn't
understand her.
They met on the veranda
of Yolanda's
hacienda.

Yolanda winked,
Miranda blinked,
sans clothes
on the veranda,
when suddenly Miranda
began to understand her.

Entwined
on the veranda
of Yolanda's
hacienda,
Miranda and Yolanda
made a heaven
out of hell.

Gordon Jackson

Ripples In A Pool

Love was made to touch our hearts
Like ripples in a pool,
A comfort sent to those in need
When fate seems harsh and cruel.

A kindly word, a gentle hand,
Will spread the love around,
We pass our strength and faith to those
Whose loss is so profound.

To know our loved one's in a place
Where pain and fear are gone,
Is balm upon the wounded heart
And helps us to move on.

For only those who've suffered loss
Can ease our heartache sore,
And help us make our memories
A lasting treasure-store.

So share your grief, and weep your tears
Until the smiles return,
Then reach out to console a friend,
And hearts will grow and learn.

Brenda Maple

Answers On A Postcard

How do you fall out of love?
Answers on a postcard,
Please.

Go now, to a wild place,
Where huge waves lash stark cliffs
And diamond spray makes rainbows,
Where tempests storm, gulls cry
And myriad sea pinks dance to the wind's song.

Go now, to a quiet place,
To a beach deserted,
Where small, scuttling creatures
Seek refuge in the sand
And the whispering sea laps gently on the shore.

Go now, to the vibrant city,
Where traffic roars and birds are hushed,
Where the hustle and bustle of life,
Frenzied by night as by day,
Dulls the innermost yearnings of the heart.

Go now, to an ancient place,
Where proud ruins speak
Volumes of past lives,
Where lizards lounge beneath stones,
Tall columns stand majestic
In a tapestry of summer flowers.

Go now, to a place of peace.
Walk through an old churchyard,
Where each crumbling stone tells its story
Of a life spent,
Good or ill,
In pursuit of happiness.

Go now, and stay,
Until you have drawn comfort from the wind's soft kiss,
Seen fragments of your broken dreams fuse
Into one glorious rainbow's arc,
Watched your tears become part of the restless ocean,
Known freedom

As the gently rolling hills
Cradled your soul.

How do you fall out of love?

Answers
    On a postcard,
        Please.

Norma Fraser Reid

Love's Destiny

What am I searching for?
I can't find you
I must be looking for a love so true

Don't know what I want
I don't seem to care
All I know is you aren't there

Must be searching for someone new
Hoping to find love
But what do I do?

There's no one out there
What can I do?
How do I find another love
That will be true?

Don't want to make a mistake
So I'll leave it all to fate
Or so-called destiny
Whatever will be will be.

Marie Haswell

Cornwall (1956)

The face at the window
    Was not your face
I thought it was you
    I wanted it to be
But of your features
    There was no trace

That late spring morning
    So many years ago
As we climbed the hill
    For a view of the Hoe
All we could hear
    Was the seabirds' shrill
And the waves beating down
    On the rocks below

As we sat in the sun
    Near the cliff-top path
By primrose and wild violet
    You said you loved me
Would never leave me
    You were gone
Before the sun had set

So where are you now
    I miss you so
And retrace those steps
    Of long ago

I'll look for you round every corner
    Study every stranger's face
Search high and low each new day dawning
    Until I find you once again.

C M Lewin

Too Weary By Sweetness

Who will watch over you
As you dream the night away?
Who will envy moonbeams
As they softly kiss your face?
Who will feel the warmth
From their embrace?
Who will guide the shooting stars
That quickly fall your way?
Who will hold your hand
As you walk the Milky Way?
Who will compare your beauty
To the wonders of that way?

J E Gobbin

Fix Your Eyes

Fix your eyes, fix your eyes
Fix your eyes onto mine
For the beauty I see in you
What you think, what you know
What you do, what you say
Because I love you so

Fix your hearts, fix your hearts
Fix your heart into mine
And I will enter your love
What you think, what you know
What you do, what you say
Because I love you so

Fix your mind, fix your mind
So you can control mine
Because of my love for you
What you think, what you know
What you do, what you say
Because I love you so.

Ray Duncan

Dreams

In my dreams I can see you, although you are far away,
you are constantly in my thoughts every minute of the day.
In my dreams I can see you, walking on hot desert sand,
my arms reach out to touch you and take you by the hand.

In my dreams we are bathing, in the sun's hot thermal rays,
laughing and frolicking about, in those warm summer days.
In my dreams there is beauty and bewilderment all abound,
as exotic blooms and orchids, are in flower all over the ground.

In my dreams the sky is glistening and not all full of woe,
colours blending together to form a beautiful curved rainbow.
In my dreams it's getting cold now as autumn fades away,
snowflakes are falling quite heavily, out riding on our sleigh.

In my dreams we are walking by woods and ice-bound streams,
your face is very clear now, but it only happens in my dreams.
My dreams have started fading, as the visions just mist away,
I hope the Lord will spare you, and return home to me I pray.

Raymond Thomas Edwards

For The Duration . . .

Loving Memories

A crisp, cold March day in Aberdeen with blue sky and sunshine
The luxury limousine moves slowly now
So smart, solemn the driver
My beloved brother Paul coffined with lilies.

Approaching the chapel, white and purple crocus
Snow cascading the ground
Our car stops while the coffin is placed on dais
The minister, so composed
Kilted Eric Whyte relates stories of yesteryear.
The final blessing and hymn
I trace the rainbow through the rain
Oh, love that wilt not let me go.

Escorted now back to the car, emotions high
Meeting grieving friends in the cricket club
So many people who knew me as a child.

Now seated in aeroplane heading to Gatwick
The stewards' very professional
Remembering memories I shared with Paul
Will heal my sorrowful heart
Happy in life that shall endless be.

Patricia Turpin

Can't Let Go
(Dedicated to Claire)

Time is moving fast to the point of no return
I'm reaching for tomorrow, leaving bridges that I've burned
Here I stand alone with my back against the wall
Tortured by your memory and the feelings I recall

Everywhere I turn I see shadows on the wall
A silhouette of sorrow of a man who had it all
Your kiss forever haunts me like a ghost out of the past
It's peaceful for a moment but it never seems to last

I'm getting tired of living with these questions in my mind
Is it hopeful to imagine or just a waste of time
For now I go on dreaming, that's what's keeping me alive
But dreams won't last forever, tell me, how will I survive?

I can't seem to get over you
No matter where I go
No matter what I do
The wall of denial
Has broken in two
And I can't seem to get over you.

Steven Hunter

For The Duration . . .

Two Flames Are One

Shouldn't love be a pleasure
and not a pain
it should be called madness
it drives you insane

Two flickering flames
candles alight
visible chemistry
glowing so bright

But love can be a burden
stuck in your heart
prodding inside you
like a dart

The candle wax melts
strong still is the flame
they mingle in pleasure
feeling the same

Love can make us feel good
love also hurts
from serious partners
to harmless flirts

The flames are now one
their love truly shines
merging their bodies
the wax intertwines.

Paola Borella

For You

Whenever I walk with you I feel
A sense of security rare.
A pleasant peace of mind and soul
With the rest of the world a background
For our united thoughts.
No need for a conversation lengthy
A squeeze of the hand, a look in the eye,
Can mean so much more than words.
We can interpret when no other can
For do we not think as one?
My thoughts when with you are of higher things
A deeper sense of religion
You have refreshed in my mind
That which I learnt as a child
And have oft' struggled hard to remember
You have brought me back when I would have strayed
With an influence great on my being.
Together we'll tread the pathway of life
And guide shall we be to each other
And whatever may come to pass or to stay
I will love you, only you and no other.

Phyllis Everett

A Moment
(Dedicated to James Prosser)

A moment with you brings a smile
A moment with you brings a tear
A moment with you brightens the day
A moment without you, dark clouds are in the way
A moment to talk to you stops me feeling blue
A moment without your voice, don't know what to do
A moment to think of you, my heart skips a beat
A moment without a thought of you makes me weak
A moment to look into your eye makes me reach the
                                          heavens in the sky
A moment without seeing you makes me want to cry
A moment to say, 'Hello, how do you feel? Where did you go?'
A moment without knowing really hurts me so
A moment with a hug makes me not want to let go
A moment without your arms around me tight makes my day
                                          turn into a long, lonely night
A moment to kiss your lips makes me shudder and feel like bliss
A moment without your kiss, it's you I really miss
A moment to say I love you makes my heart beat fast
A moment without the words you speak wants the day to go past
But always and forever each moment our love to last.

Michelle Barnes

Signorinas Ask For Dates

Aware that men have not the nerve
to make the courtship openings,
Italian misses seem to know
if alcohol's inspired a beau
to start romantic happenings.

Boys wish there was a thicker line
between normal advances, and
harassment, in the dating rules.
Love instructions aren't taught in schools,
however much parents demand.

Unless they're easy, girls prefer
men's minds to stay above the belt.
To keep too-eager hopes in check,
they'll dress in clothes with a high neck . . .
till too much summer heat is felt.

Gillian Fisher

Guardian

My beautiful friend
Stay with me tonight
And we can talk for a while, if that's alright
We can talk of our youth and the tricks we played
We can talk of our future and the plans we've made
My beautiful friend
Stay with me tonight
And we can watch the dancing firelight
We can watch the stars dance above
We can admire each other and fall in love
My beautiful friend
Stay with me tonight
And we can fill our minds with love's delight
We can fill our hearts with happiness
We can fill our lives with a soft caress.

Anita Marlene Stridgen

For The Duration . . .

Unconditional

My love for you is unconditional

The love that I have for you
Just seems to grow and grow
As the days pass by
My feelings for you just seem to blossom.

My love for you is unconditional
Unconditional, unconditional
My love is unconditional.

There's been many times when we've argued
There's been many times when we've cried
I love being with you
I still have the same feelings
Because . . .

My love for you is unconditional
It will always be the same
It will always, it will always
It will always be the same.

Whenever I'm upset
Whenever I'm in trouble
If I need some help
You are there for me
I'm also there for you.

That's because our love for each other is unconditional
We will never, we will never
We will never fall apart.

All the obstacles that are put in our way
We will see it through together
We are sewn at the hip
We're together forever.

Robert Bradley

Eulogy Of Love (Part One)

. . . One touch by the aberrant wings, became
captive to foul play of insobriety. Strayed
into a cacophony of perilous sounds, and
erratic forks, exhibiting a peculiar insanity.
Averse to the essence of love.

She brashfully spoke. 'Is this not but a vibe,
of an intangible emotion, characterised
through, a reckless devotion?'

Opulently portrays her unfettered hysteria,
suggestive whispers, and devouring exterior.
The fledgling wings temporarily succumb'd
to subliminal message piercing the heart,
only to be immortalised, by the senseless
dove . . .

Adam Imaan

For The Lovers

Lover come closer - look over your shoulder
I'm feeling your presence - your heart grows in essence
I'm feeling your soul - surround me as I fall
Never has my mind - been left open and blind
to your lover's call - from the night till the morn
I need what you give - to help me to live
this pain is my pleasure - for your heart to treasure
so if I should lift - your angelic gift
remind me to ponder - your glorious wonder
or never be shaken - by my heart you've taken
now remember this - as your heart calls in bliss
to take pleasure with pain - as you echo my name.

Ade Horton

Valentine's Day

I dreamed of you last night.
Even though I remembered on waking
that you are the other side of the world,
I still felt a closeness and joy,
because in my dream you came to me,
planted a special kiss on my cheek
and said, 'I love you, and that is forever.'
That was my only consolation,
knowing that you are still thinking of me
with that old comforting way of yours.
All those thousands of miles between us
shrank to nothing.
My morning was lifted to unreal heights,
as memories were rekindled of happier days
together in the garden or by the fireside.
We planted for the future, you and me,
with images of next year's daffodils,
and Easter Evensong a glorious hour,
to give us hope and happiness and love
enough for both, with plenty more to give away.
While we are apart, my Valentine,
I mark the days off on the calendar,
and practise all those lovely words to say
to you, when you return for real.

J M White

At First Sight

At first sight man or maid encounter love's light.
In their eyes appears a sparkle, swift as
That old Derby winner, Arkle!
It is a sensation warm, a feeling to charm,
Nothing to startle, it is a tryst not to be missed.
One that should be on everyone's list.
Love, the force to unitise a couple to their surprise,
One they cannot disguise, so fortunate they thus relate,
Both realise. To each they give their heart
Swearing never to part, but science declares the heart is
Simply a pump, vital though, if life is not to slump.
However unclear, it is a nice idea.
So beginning the search again, conclude
It is all in the brain! There must be a
Sexual attraction, impelling action spot,
As like as not! If so it must be hot, for
It works like a shot! Drawing the sexes ever closer,
Few there are who answer, 'No Sir!'
So for the gift of love we should all thank God.

Mr G Watkins

Shadows

In the darkness of the night
Or the dawning of the day.
In the time it takes to wake
When you wish that you could sleep
The memories that will not leave your mind,
Paint the pictures that efface the normality of life,
To remind you, you are always on your own.
You can laugh for just a moment,
On the journey of the day
Smile and talk and play your part,
But your loneliness is like a burden, that you cannot put aside,
For the one you love has died,
Like the lightning in a storm
And the trauma lingers on.
They say that time heals all
Careless words,
Don't they know your world has changed,
Can never be the same.
Be brave and start anew
New friends, new outlook
Is what you need, they say
The sadness hides within, in the shadows.

June Holmes

Togetherness

Twenty-three years we shared together
Promised when old we'd help each other.
Then suddenly came that awful blow
That soon your breath would cease to flow.

Precious moments were ticking away
Life slipping painfully by each day.
Hiding my tears behind closed door
A smiling face I bravely wore.

Love of my life you left too soon
Now into old age alone is my doom.
Being together whatever the weather
Shared those last months lovingly together.

I shared the pain your illness made
Holding your hand as in bed you laid.
We whispered words of love sincere
From me you hid your thoughts and fear.

Dearest one, those precious moments -
I tried to soothe away your torments.
With suffering showing in your eyes
I conveyed my love would never die.

Valerie Tedder

For The Duration . . .

Maybe

When the clouds roll by will my sun ever shine?
For we are so far apart when you could be mine

We have years of joy and love to share
But sometimes I wonder if you really care

Will you be my love?
Will you be my life
Through times of happiness, trouble and strife?

As the years fly by and time takes its toll
Let's get it together before we're too old

If the years were younger and the time was right
I wouldn't think twice, I would make you my wife

It's all a dream or so it would seem
But it could come true if I were with you.

B J Shire

Thoughts Of Love

At the closing of the day I especially think of thee;
At the closing of the day wilt thou also think of me?
Our thoughts will then become entwined –
Thine with mine and mine with thine.

Although alone, we are together,
The thoughts of love our hearts doth tether,
And no force on Earth can that bond sever.
We then drift softly into sleep –
Warm thoughts of love in our hearts to keep.

On into dreams we as one become,
Lost in love's fusion we both succumb,
Lest we should too soon to wake,
And feel our hearts divellicate.

Still I cradle thee through the night's dark storms,
Till the rising sun marks a new day born.
I live the day and think of thee;
Dost thou live thy day and think of me?

Roger Oldfield

For The Duration . . .

Young At Heart

When we met, I breathed again
When we kissed, you eased my pain
When we danced, full animation
When we alone sat, anticipation
When we said, goodnight in street
We then agreed, again to meet

When we met for second time
Inner thoughts all so sublime
We held hands in our element
Risible with nervous excitement
Coy glances, smiles, little talk
Cuddled, as by shallow river walk
Saw our reflection in clear water
I was someone's son, you someone's daughter
Respectful behaviour show towards you
For your trust in me, respect is due
To keep happy, feel alive, 'I need you woman'
Heard you whisper, abide! 'I need you man'
We have waited too long to hesitate
I want you now! It's desperate
Our parents? Long past on I'm afraid
Lie together in well-tended grave
Oh! Of you they would approve
Be so proud to know we love
Yes! Guessed right, we're not young anymore
Years coming up towards threescore
Shocked dear reader? Oh heart of steel
Love is not only for young ones
But how young one feels.

Arthur S Waller

Smitten

Lunchtime finds him
sauntering through town
back to the office.
Grey suit, jacket loose,
newspaper under his arm,
hands deep down in his pockets.
A breeze flies his tie,
messes up his hair
and polishes off his whistling.

If you watch, you should
catch him trying out
a stylish touch or two
of clever footwork -
double-steps to pot a stone,
a little detour sideways
just to cuff a weed
or make some other
careless happy declaration.

Erica Warburton

I Love You

Did I one day love you
And did tomorrow become the day after that?
Now yesterday is so far behind me
Is love still within my heart?
Only now we are apart
Matter and time are together
Sadness is in my heart
Tears are in my eyes
Reminitions are in my mind
The wisdom of you and I
Is blind to this day.

Patrick Joseph Ryan

For The Duration . . .

My Pet

For years I had a pet and loved him dearly,
And I do know, he loved me too,
My faithful pet was neither dog nor cat,
Budgie or cockatoo.

He never left my side if he could help it,
The devotion in his eyes matched only mine,
He did his best to please and sometimes was a tease,
But with him, I was always on cloud nine.

From the start we were meant for each other,
He was prepared to guard me with his life,
And when together we vowed to love and cherish,
I just knew that everything was right.

But now, I shed a tear, for my pet is no longer here,
And how I long for his touch and warm embrace,
For my pet was my dear devoted husband,
And no other could ever take his place.

Dorothy M Titley

Lament

My sun makes a break for it;
running to catch your moon;
but then night comes between us –
as it always does.

Your moon slips away from her stars;
running to embrace my sun;
only for dawn to come between us –
like it always does.

Are we destined, my love,
never to meet in the same sky?

Robert Shreeve

Romance In Your Latter Years

To fall in love the second time round,
New life has been found;
An experience of mature people falling in love,
It is not just a monopoly of the young.

Parts of your body you thought had faded away,
Are revived to live another day;
He sees in her the charm of inward glow,
She sees in him only things she can know.

You are never past the age of romance,
Why not give love a chance;
You can still kiss and cuddle,
Why be depressed with your life in a muddle.

As you get older you may not be what you used to be,
But there is still hope as long as you have the chemistry;
Be quixotic, go for it today,
To waste your last chance of love is to waste your life away.

Love that is mature is better than vintage wine,
It will make you feel an age that always ends in nine;
Late in life you have spring fever,
You can never leave her.

Cynical will talk, the young will laugh,
Some will say at their age they are daft;
But those in love will have a treasure,
They will end their days enjoying the pleasure.

Robin R Robinson

Desertion

Looking at the far horizon
Brightly red at start of day
Peering quietly out the window
Right across the peaceful bay.

Not a boat is on the water
Not a soul is on the shore
Just the gulls, their plaintive crying
Like the day that went before.

Sitting thinking of what has been
All the good and bad that's passed
Wondering what the future will bring
Lost the love I thought would last.

Now the road ahead is empty
So much love I had to give
Saddened by the way you left me
Hope one day I can forgive.

Just an empty feeling inside
Sleepless nights are many now
Tears that fill the eyes so often
Only questions, why and how?

Marje Dale

Love's Journey

I've felt the pain of lost love,
As deep as any sword,
When a careless heart has broken
Love's umbilical cord.

Felt abandoned as a kitten
Left out in the snow;
Cold and desolate and lost
With no warm place to go.

Then the dearest, kindest man
Came into my life,
Wanting one thing only;
For me to be his wife.

We've now been married forty years
Contented, still in love,
Like a foot to a comfy slipper
Or a hand to a well-used glove.

Now settling into later life
By the firelight's soft glow
I sometimes think of those old loves
And the heartache long ago.

Then I look at the one that endured,
The love that was meant to be,
Knowing till death I'll be there for him
As he will be there for me.

Shirley Brooks

Love For A Lifetime

I'm sitting alone by the fireside
Thinking of good times gone by,
Wondering why you had to leave me
Glad of memories which still make me cry.

That night we first met, how could I forget?
Saturday night when the cinema drew.
Was it sheer fate that I arrived late,
And was shown to a seat right next to you?

Sherlock Holmes was solving a crime
With disturbing scenes most of the time
'I'm so sorry,' I said, when I grabbed hold of your palm
'It's OK,' you replied, 'it will help you stay calm.'

I wondered why I'd not seen you before
And thinking I would like to see you some more
When next night, on a bridge watching the fish
You were suddenly there and I got my wish.

We began dating, taking a chance
This was the start of a lasting romance.
Tender love and happiness grew
Talking any troubles away with a kiss or two.

When you asked me to marry you, 'I will,' my heart sang,
I was on cloud nine when the church bells rang.
This magical day, we'd become man and wife,
Vows made to each other, sealed 'our love for life'.

We had been wed for thirty-four years
When you woke up not feeling too well,
You said at the time you had pain in your chest
And it was really giving you hell!

Later that day you were whisked away
To a place that's far better so they say.
So many memories you left with me
My heart still aches when I turn the key.

Lucy Mary Dean

Tanya, I Do Love You So Very Much

Tanya I do love you so very much.
I also love your company and your sexy touch!
I know I keep saying this again and again,
But I always want to see you so, *when?*

You are special, loving, caring and very kind,
Helpful, wonderful and you've got an intelligent mind!
I wish I could have you 24 hours a day,
Doing what other couples do . . . hooray!

We could go to concerts, galleries, plays,
Films and always have fun,
Stay in, watch TV/DVDs, cuddles, sex, regularly,
And all these *should* be done!
Maybe we could go to quizzes, at the local pubs,
In-between days, you go to Guides/Brownies, clubs.

I *H*ope *O*ur *L*ove *L*asts *A*nd *N*ever *D*ies,
And we never ever make each other really cry.
*I T*rust *A*nd *L*ove *Y*ou, forever . . .
Oh, very sexy, loving partner!

Barry Ryan

Untitled

Remember me as winter sun,
with tender hints of gold,
remember me as that special one,
the hand you had to hold,
remember when we said goodbye,
I cried a million tears,
remember what you mean to me,
our love throughout the years,
remember now that I am gone,
that soon we'll meet again,
my love for you is forever,
a story never to end.

Jennifer Clare Kerr

The Love Of My Life

He was the love of my life
And my best friend.
We thought our world
Would never end.
Those special smiles
And jokes we shared.
The loving touch
To show we cared.
But the surgeon's knife
Ripped deep inside
And the love of my life
Slowly died.

Angy Lindsay

Forward Press Information

We hope you have enjoyed reading this book - and that you will continue to enjoy it in the coming years.

If you like reading and writing poetry drop us a line, or give us a call, and we'll send you a free information pack.

Alternatively if you would like to order further copies of this book or any of our other titles, then please give us a call or log onto our website at www.forwardpress.co.uk

Forward Press Information
Remus House
Coltsfoot Drive
Peterborough
PE2 9JX
(01733) 890099